Karen Carlson-Kreibohm

MERRY CHRISTMAS

RESOURCE BOOK
FOR USE IN SCHOOLS

Stories · Songs · Plays · Poems · Traditions
Activities · Recipes · Puzzles

Cornelsen

CONTENTS

WE WISH YOU A MERRY CHRISTMAS

Words and tune English traditional

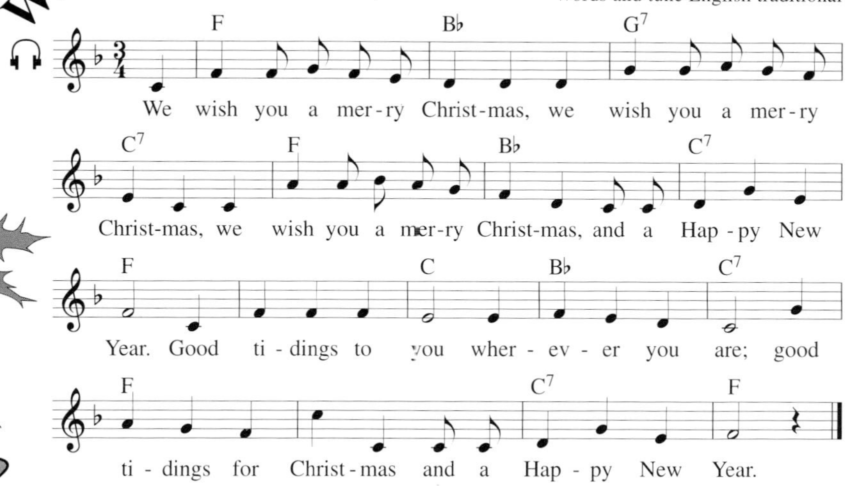

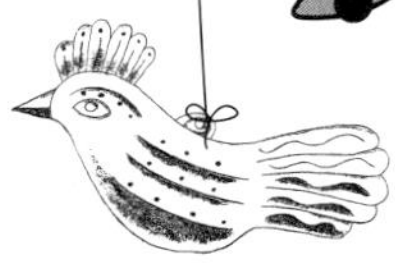

What does Christmas mean to you?

Santa on his sleigh pulled by reindeer?

Singing carols in church?

Heading for the beach on Christmas Day?

Roast turkey and Christmas pudding?

Sing hey! Sing hey!
For Christmas Day!
Twine mistletoe and holly,
For friendship glows
In winter snows
And so let's all be jolly!

Traditional Rhyme

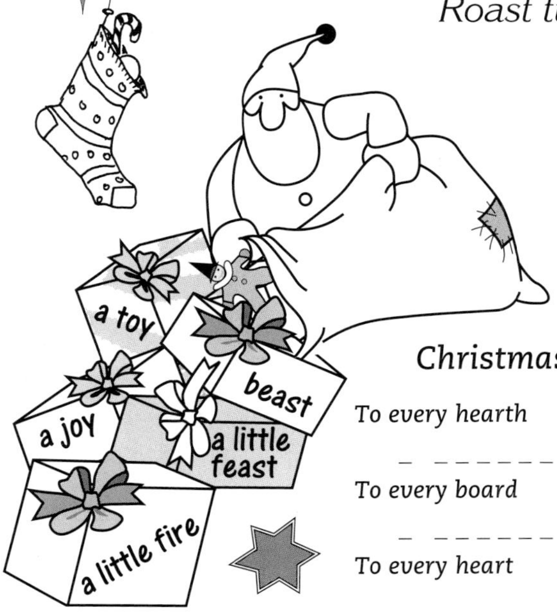

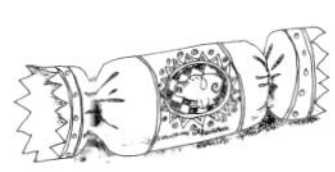

Christmas Wish

To every hearth

_ ______ ____

To every board

_ ______ _____

To every heart

_ ___

To every child

_ ___

Shelter for bird and

_____.

Rose Fyleman

Christmas Rush

tidings *(old use) – news*
twine – winden
hearth – Feuerstelle
board *(old use) – table*

I Remember

by *Dan Nukala*

I Remember

Christmas that year. I was 12.

My parents had divorced earlier that year. My mother was working three jobs each week. She was a secretary. She was a waitress at the truck stop most nights. She was a waitress in a donut shop on weekends.

I Remember

Christmas that year. I was 12.

My sister and I were in charge of the house. My mother was too tired to decorate for the holidays. We picked out the tree and hauled the decorations down from the upstairs closet. We untangled the lights and laced them through the branches. We unwrapped the glass balls and placed them carefully, balancing each side, as mother always had. We tossed the crinkled tinsel to finish the effect. And that night, when mother came home from work, we sat her down and lit the tree.
She cried.

I Remember

Christmas that year. I was 12.

My father was gone. There were no presents from him. There would be no presents from him. We did not want his presents. And we did not want his presence, either.

I Remember

Christmas that year. I was 12.

We had made paper gifts and cards at school. Angels and geometric shapes. Cotton balls and glitter on red and green paper. Long paper chains. We made popcorn balls that were hard as ice. We made cookies with raisins and chocolate chips and silver sprinkles. We made a mess of the kitchen. And when my mother came home and saw us elbow-deep in flour and sugar and cookie dough, she laughed. It was the first time she'd laughed in a long time.

I Remember

Christmas that year. I was 12.

I gave my mother a book of poems that I'd written. My sister gave her a book of her own drawings. We took old Christmas cards and made a collage for her to hang up in her office. We took oranges and spiked them with cloves so she could freshen the air in her car. We soaked cotton balls in toilet water, then sewed them into material to make sachets for her bureau drawers and closet. We bought her a fake diamond necklace at Harvey's dime store so she could look glamorous. She wore it to work the next week.

I Remember

Christmas that year. I was 12.

It snowed that year. On Christmas Eve, it snowed in huge white flakes that seemed to float for hours before they hit the ground. It was cold outside. But inside, we were very, very warm.

Create something similar by using your own memories.
– List five specific events in your life that happened at Christmastime or in the winter.
– Choose one of those events and list all the memories you have of it. Be specific. Concentrate on what you saw, smelled, touched, tasted, heard, and thought about.
– Use your memories to create an "I Remember" story.

in charge of – *responsible for* ***holidays*** – (AE) Feiertage (*Christmas and New Year*) ***to untangle*** – entwirren ***tinsel*** – Lametta ***cloves*** – Nelken ***sachet*** – [sæˈʃeɪ] Duftkissen ***bureau drawer*** – (AE) Kommodenschublade ***closet*** – (AE) Kleiderkammer ***fake*** – *not real* ***necklace*** – Kette ***dime store*** – (AE) *inexpensive department store*

No.	Greeting	Pronunciation	Language	
1	Wesołych Świąt	[vεsɔwix ˈçviɔŋt]	German	A
2	Buon Natale	[buon naˈtale]	Chinese	B
3	God Jul	[guː jyːl]	Filipino	C
4	عيد مبارك	[ˈeːd mu ˈbarak]	French	D
5	新年好	[ʃɪŋ njer hau]	Gujarati	E
6	Feliz Navidad	[feˈlɪs navɪˈdad]	Finnish	F
7	Lethabo la keresemose	[ləˈtabo lakeˈreseˈmɔse]	Korean	G
8	Mele Kalikimaka	[ˈmele kaliːkiːˈmaka]	Afrikaans	H
9	MALIGAYANG PASKO	[maligaiaŋ ˈpasko]	Dutch	I
10	Vrolijk Kerstfeest	[ˈvrolεik ˈkerstfeːst]	Greek	J
11	Честита Коледа	[ˈtʃestita ˈkɔleda]	Hawaiian	K
12	Frohe Weihnachten	[ˈfroːə ˈvainaxtən]	Bulgarian	L
13	Joyeux Noël!	[ʒwajø nɔεl]	Italian	M
14	Sretan Božić	[ˈsretan bɔzɪtʃ]	Northern-Sotho	N
15	Καλά Χριστούγεννα	[kaˈla xrɪstˈoujena]	Polish	O
16	Hyvää Joulua	[ˈhyːvεː ˈjolua]	Russian	P
17	שנה טובה	[ˈʃanato ˈva]	Spanish	Q
18	Feliz Natal	[fəˈlɪʃ nəˈtal]	Persian	R
19	С Новым Годом	[ˈsnovɪm ˈgɔː dim]	Serbo-Croatian	S
20	즐거운 성탄절	[ʃɪl go on soŋ tan ʃɔl]	Swedish	T
21	Geseënde Kersfees	[xəˈseəndə ˈkerʃfeːs]	Portuguese	U
22	સાલ મુબારક	[saːl muˈbarak]	Hebrew	V

Which greeting is in which language? Cut out the boxes and match the greetings to the languages, starting with the ones you know or can guess. Put the boxes together like dominoes in a long row.

1-O, 2-M, 3-T, 4-R, 5-B, 6-Q, 7-N, 8-K, 9-C, 10-I, 11-L, 12-A, 13-D, 14-S, 15-J, 16-F, 17-V, 18-U, 19-P, 20-G, 21-H, 22-E

CELEBRATING THE SEASON

Reports from Ireland, Australia, the USA, England and Scotland

Christmas in Ireland is brilliant fun. Normally we all pray for the good old white Christmas, but we usually end up with rain. Typical Ireland. For most people, Christmastime starts on 8th December, a holiday called the Feast of the Immaculate Conception. Most Irish put up their Christmas trees then, decorating them with stars, angels, fairy lights, the lot. The young children write to Father Christmas and ask for their gifts – and on Christmas Eve he comes to every house delivering presents to all good children. On Christmas morning we open presents and have a good Irish breakfast of hot boiled ham, bread and tea. Then we all go to Mass, where there is a crib to remind us of the birth of Jesus Christ and why we have Christmas. Christmas afternoon is usually all the families joining together. In Ireland so many of us emigrate to bigger and better countries, so Christmas is the only time we all get together.

The day after Christmas is St Stephen's Day and that's when groups of young people dress up as scarecrows, old farmers, anything at all as long as we look messy. We ride around in a trailer pulled by a tractor and stop at different houses. We sing for the people and they give us something to eat and drink and money for our youth club. This funny tradition is called "Hunting the Wren", and in the old days people carried around a dead bird on a stick, but we don't do that any more!

Christmas in Ireland is brilliant. I really would not fancy eating my Christmas dinner of turkey and ham on a hot sunny beach. I only want to ever be in Ireland for Christmas.

Becky Donoghue
Ballinderry, County Tipperary, Ireland

In Australia there are people from so many different countries who have their own customs at Christmastime. In my family, for example, we have "Santa Barbara" in early December. If you've been a good little girl or boy, you get sweets in your shoe the next morning. But if you've been bad, you get rocks. (I always got sweets, of course ...)

Like in England, Santa Claus brings presents during the night on Christmas Eve, but on Christmas morning, as soon as the presents are opened, Australians head down to the beach to meet friends and have some mince pies with champagne or Australian wine. People swim, play volleyball, get a suntan and have a good time. You also see lots of men dressed up like Santa Claus walking along the beach, sometimes playing guitars and singing carols, just for fun.

I'm from Sydney, and the big event for us is on Boxing Day, the 26th. Everyone goes to the harbour, which is completely packed full of sailing boats and yachts starting off on the big Sydney to Hobart boat race.

Australians are very open, very friendly, and nobody is an outsider. Christmastime isn't just for the family, but it's a time to get together with friends and have a barbecue and go surfing or sailing. Sometimes you see plastic snow in the shop windows, but I think most Australians, like me, would rather have the 25 degree weather and the beach at Christmas.

Bronwyn Darnoc
Sydney, Australia

My father is Lutheran and my mother is Jewish, so naturally we are a busy family in December, when we celebrate both Christmas and Hanukkah, sometimes within the same week. At Hanukkah we have a menorah, a special candleholder. For each of the eight nights of Hanukkah, we light one more candle and enjoy a candlelight dinner. Sometimes we eat latkes, the traditional potato pancakes with apple sauce. Each evening we also sing prayers in Hebrew. My parents give my sister Emily and me a little gift on each of the eight nights, but they usually save the big gifts for Christmas. My grandparents from New York often visit us during Hanukkah and they always bring presents too.

Although I was brought up Jewish and celebrated my Bar Mitzvah when I was thirteen, our family rarely goes to the synagogue. The Jewish holidays are a time for me to celebrate my Judaism. Even without the presents, I would still be excited about the religious idea of the miracle that happened long ago and that we celebrate at Hanukkah. For me, Hanukkah is a time of joy, whether the joy comes from presents, celebration, or just some evenings together with the whole family.

Elliott Green
Evanston, Illinois, USA

I'm from a little farming community in the northwest of England and one thing I always enjoy about Christmas is going carol singing. A few days before Christmas, before people get too busy with their turkeys and everything, about thirty of us from all different age groups get together to go from house to house singing and collecting money for the church.

Santa Claus opening his sack on a beach in Australia, where Christmas comes in the middle of summer

An American house all dressed up for Christmas

We don't practise first, and there are lots of people who can't sing very well, but that doesn't matter at all and it's always a load of laughs. I dust off my trumpet once a year for it, and others play guitars and mouth-organs. We like to do carols like "God Rest Ye Merry, Gentlemen" and we take special requests too. The dear old ladies always want us to do "Silent Night".

Since the farms are so far apart, we all get into cars to get from one old farmhouse to the next. It often happens that part of the group gets lost on the dark country roads and then we have two or three carol singing groups instead of one, but that's part of the fun.

We always end up in a pub. We're careful to choose one where they will be nice and give us mince pies and mulled wine. That feels really good after wandering around in the cold.

Tim Moss
Cockermouth, England

In Scotland children look forward to Christmas, of course, because that's when they get presents from Santa Claus, but traditionally, Hogmanay, as we call New Year's Eve, is an equally important day in Scotland.

In Edinburgh and bigger towns there are huge street parties all night long with carnival rides and games. There aren't any fireworks, though, because in Britain they're only allowed once a year, on Guy Fawkes' Day. In my little town it's quieter, but for kids it's still very special to be able to stay up till 2 am, or at least to try to stay awake that long.

The TV is always on and there are lots of shows with traditional Scottish dancers and singers. Everyone waits for the chimes of Big Ben down in London to strike 12 and then we all link arms and sing the traditional old Scottish song, "Auld Lang Syne". We always have shortbread to eat, and while the adults drink whisky or sherry, the kids drink ginger wine. That's a very sweet Scottish drink that has such a strong spicy taste that it burns your tongue. In fact, as little kids we thought it must be alcohol because the taste was so terribly nippy.

After midnight people go "first-footing". That means they visit neighbours and relatives to wish everyone a happy New Year and bring something for good luck, like a piece of coal or some salt as well as a bottle to share. After having a drink and some shortbread or fruitcake, they move on to the next house and keep doing this until 3 or 4 in the morning. In Scotland we have two bank holidays afterwards, January 1 and January 2, so people have time to recover from all this.

Linda Wilson
Ayr, Scotland

"The stockings were hung by the chimney with care, in hopes that St Nicholas soon would be there ..."

At Christmastime, Texans try to turn many things into 'Texmas'. In the tourist area of Dallas there's a Texas longhorn all dressed up for Christmas with a red coat and hat and jingle bells and you can sit on him and have your picture taken. There's also a huge Christmas tree outside with giant presents around it, and an outdoor ice-skating rink, refrigerated from underneath, since December is usually very mild here.

Some people spend thousands of dollars to decorate the outside of their houses, covering every tree and bush with lights. Last year one house turned itself into a gingerbread house with giant lollipops and candy canes on the lawn. Another one had Santa climbing a giant oil well. Moving parts are a big deal. You see lots of little elves hammering away on toys, etc. Sometimes traffic is backed up for at least 30–45 minutes because so many people want to drive by the decorated houses.

Texans also love parties, and the nice thing about Dallas is that everyone is welcome, whether or not you know the people. I even went to a party once at Southfork Ranch, where the TV series Dallas was filmed. Everyone was dressed in velvet or some form of glitter. Carriage rides were available and you could have your picture taken sitting in a white sleigh with lots of white lights and fake snow. Beautiful!

Lots of people have their picture taken sitting on Santa's lap too. Mostly little kids, of course, who visit Santa at the shopping mall and tell him what they want for Christmas. But my friends and I like to sit on his lap too. At my college there's a huge statue of our founder, Judge Baylor, and we always dress him up like Santa and then sit on his lap and have our pictures taken.

Christina Starace
Dallas, Texas, USA

Becky (Ireland): ***Immaculate Conception*** – Unbefleckte Empfängnis (*Catholic holiday*) ***the lot*** – (infml) *everything* ***Mass*** – Messe ***scarecrow*** – Vogelscheuche ***wren*** – Zaunkönig

Bronwyn (Australia): ***barbecue*** – Grillparty

Elliott (USA): ***Hanukkah*** ('– – –) ***menorah*** (– '– –) ***Bar Mitzvah*** – *ceremony when a boy becomes a full member of the Jewish community* ***synagogue*** ('– – –)

Tim (England): ***mulled*** – *mixed with sugar and spices and heated*

Linda (Scotland): ***Hogmanay*** ('– – –)

Christina (USA): ***gingerbread*** – Lebkuchen ***lollipop*** – Lutscher ***lawn*** – *grass* ***big deal*** – *important, "in"* ***velvet*** – Samt ***carriage*** – Kutsche ***fake*** – *not real*

חנוכה

O HANUKKAH

HANUKKAH

The Jewish "Festival of Lights" is celebrated for eight nights in December. Over 2000 years ago a Syrian-Greek king tried to force the Jews to give up their religion. They fought a battle and got back their temple. There was only enough oil for the temple lights (which were meant to burn all the time) to burn for one day, but by a miracle, the lights burned for eight days.

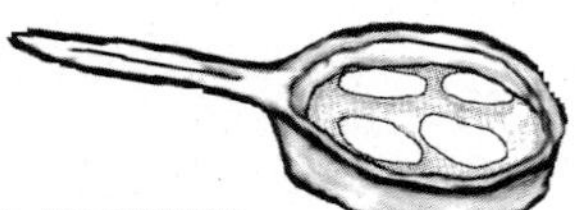

LATKES

3 potatoes, grated
1 small onion, grated
2 tablespoons flour
2 eggs, salt and pepper
Mix everything and fry in hot oil until golden brown. Serve with apple sauce or sour cream. (Makes about 16 pancakes.)

HANUKKAH-MENORAH – special candleholder for eight candles plus the *shamash*, the "servant" candle, used to light the others.

Jewish Folk Tune, English words by Judith Eisenstein

No Hanukkah celebration is complete without a **DREIDEL**, a spinning top with four sides and a Hebrew letter on each side. Players get an equal number of pennies (or nuts or sweets) and put one penny in the "pot" in the center. Take turns spinning the *dreidel*. Hebrew letter *nun* (Jiddish *nikhts*) = get nothing, *heh* (half) = take half the pot, *shin* (*shtell*) = put one in pot, *gimel* (*gants*) = take whole pot. After a gimel, each player puts one coin in the pot to begin again. You can make a *dreidel* from a little square box or the cup of an egg carton. Write a letter on each side and stick a pencil or large nail through the bottom.

Originally from Eastern Europe, the **HORA** is danced at Jewish festivals. Dancers form a circle and put their hands on each other's shoulders.

1) Step right with right foot
2) Place left foot behind right foot
3) Step right with right foot
4) Hop on right foot
5) Step left with left foot
6) Hop on left foot

JOHN LENNON

HAPPY XMAS (WAR IS OVER)

words and music by
John Lennon and
Yoko Ono, 1971

So this is Xmas and
what have you done?

Another year over,
a new one just begun;
And so this is Xmas,
I hope you have fun
The near and the dear ones
The old and the young.

A merry, merry Xmas
And a happy New Year,
Let's hope it's a good one
without any fear.

And so this is Xmas
for weak and for strong,
The rich and the poor ones,
the road is so long.
And so, happy Xmas
for black and for white
For the yellow and red ones,
let's stop all this fight.

A merry, merry Xmas
And a happy New Year
Let's hope it's a good one
without any fear.

(War is over if you want it,
war is over now.)

Why Xmas?

There are two reasons why some people write Xmas instead of Christmas, an historical reason and a practical reason. The historical reason is that the Greek letter X (chi) is the first letter in the Greek word for Christ. Since at least as far back as 1100, English writers followed a practice which had been used in Latin manuscripts. They wrote X as an abbreviation for Christ as well as Xnity, Xn and Xmas as short forms for Christianity, Christian and Christmas.

Most English speakers today, however, are not aware of this historical reason and often assume that Xmas was invented by modern advertisement writers as a shorter, easier form of Christmas. Xmas is often used in informal writing and on signs where it's necessary to save space.

While Xmas is very common and practical, some people think it's a lazy habit and others object to "crossing out" the name of Christ. There's a slogan "Put Christ back in Christmas."

When reading, Xmas is pronounced like Christmas and not "eks-mas", unless one wants to emphasize that the form Xmas was used.

ADRIAN MOLE'S

Adrian Mole is probably the best-known teenager in Britain. Since his diary was first published in 1981, over five million copies have been sold and there is also a TV version of the story. Although the author, Sue Townsend, is the mother of four children, she says Adrian is her own creation and not based on any of her own kids.

Adrian thinks he's an undiscovered poet and intellectual and he is in love with Pandora, a girl at his school. Another important person in his life is 89-year-old Bert, a man he visits regularly as part of a community service project.

Saturday, December 19th

I've got no money for Christmas presents. But I have made my Christmas list in case I find ten pounds in the street.

Pandora – Big bottle of Chanel No. 5 (£ 1.50)
Mother – Egg-timer (75p)
Father – Bookmark (38p)
Grandma – Packet of J cloths (45p)
Dog – Dog chocolates (45p)
Bert – 20 Woodbines (95p)
Auntie Susan – Tin of Nivea (60p)
Sabre – Box of Bob Martins, small (39p)
Nigel – Family box of Maltesers (34p)
Miss Elf – Oven-glove (home-made)

Tuesday, December 22nd

School was closed this morning because the teachers could not manage to get in on time because of the snow. That will teach them to live in old mill houses and windmills out in the country! Miss Elf lives with a West Indian in a terraced house in the town, so she bravely turned out to prepare for the school concert in the afternoon.

The school orchestra was a disaster! My mother said, "When are they going to stop tuning up and start playing?" I told her that they had just played a Mozart horn concerto. That made my mother and father and Pandora's mother and father start laughing in a very unmannerly fashion.

The Dumbo class got up and sang a few boring old carols. Barry Kent sang all the vulgar versions (I know because I was watching his lips). Then it was the interval and time for me to change into my white T-shirt-and-Wranglers Joseph costume. The tension backstage was electric. I stood in the wings (a theatrical term – it means the side of the stage) and watched the audience filing back into their places. Then the music from *Close Encounters* boomed out over the stereo speakers, and the curtains opened on an abstract manger and I just had time to whisper to Pandora "Break a leg, darling", before Miss Elf pushed us out into the lights. My performance was brilliant! I really got under the skin of Joseph, but Pandora was less good. She forgot to look tenderly at Jesus/Peter Brown.

The three punks/wise men made too much noise with their chains and spoiled my speech about the Middle East situation, and the angels representing Mrs Thatcher got hissed by the audience so loudly that their spoken chorus about unemployment was wasted.

Still, all in all, it was well received by the audience. Mr Scruton got up and made a hypocritical speech about "a brave experiment" and "Miss Elf's tireless work behind the scenes", and then we all sang "We wish you a Merry Christmas"!

Driving home in the car my father said, "That was the funniest Nativity play I have ever seen. Whose idea was it to turn it into a comedy!" I didn't reply. It wasn't a comedy.

Wednesday, December 23rd

9 am Only two shopping days left for Christmas and I am still penniless. I have made a Blue Peter oven-glove for Miss Elf, but in order to give it to her in time for Christmas I will have to go into the ghetto and risk getting mugged.

I will have to go out carol singing, there is nothing else I can do to raise finance.

10 pm Just got back from carol singing. The suburban houses were a dead loss. People shouted. "Come back at Christmas", without even opening the door. My most appreciative audience were the drunks staggering in and out of the Black Bull. Some of them wept openly at the beauty of my solo rendition of "Silent Night". I must say that I presented a touching picture as I stood in the snow with my young face lifted to the heavens ignoring the scenes of drunken revelry around me.

I made £ 3.13 ½ plus an Irish tenpence and a Guinness bottletop. I'm going out again tomorrow. I will wear my school uniform, it should be worth a few extra quid.

Thursday, December 24th

Took Bert's Woodbines round to the home. Bert is hurt because I haven't been to see him. He said he didn't want to spend Christmas with a lot of malicious old women. Him and Queenie are causing a scandal. They are unofficially engaged. They have got their names on the same ashtray. I have invited Bert and Queenie for Christmas Day. My mother doesn't know yet but I'm sure she won't mind, we have got a big turkey. I sang a few carols for the old ladies. I made two pounds eleven pence out of them so I went to Woolworth's to buy Pandora's Chanel No. 5. They hadn't got any so I bought her an underarm deodorant instead.

CHRISTMAS

An excerpt from the book
The Secret Diary of Adrian Mole, aged 13 ¾
by Sue Townsend

The house looks dead clean and sparkling, there is a magic smell of cooking and satsumas in the air. I have searched around for my presents but they are not in the usual places. I want a racing bike, nothing else will please me. It's time I was independently mobile.

11 *pm* Just got back from the Black Bull. Pandora came with me, we wore our school uniforms and reminded all the drunks of their own children. They coughed up conscience money to the tune of twelve pounds fifty-seven! So we are going to see a pantomime on Boxing Day and we will have a family bar of Cadbury's Dairy Milk each!

Friday, December 25th

CHRISTMAS DAY
Got up at *5 am* to have a ride on my racing bike. My father paid for it with American Express. I couldn't ride it far because of the snow, but it didn't matter. I just like looking at it. My father had written on the gift tag attached to the handlebars, "Don't leave it out in the rain this time" – as if I would!

My parents had severe hangovers, so I took them breakfast in bed and gave them my presents at the same time. My mother was overjoyed with her egg-timer and my father was equally delighted with his book-mark, in fact everything was going OK until I casually mentioned that Bert and Queenie were my guests for the day, and would my father mind getting out of bed and picking them up in his car.

The row went on until the lousy Sugdens arrived. My grandma and grandad Sugden and Uncle Dennis and his wife Marcia and their son Maurice all look the same, as if they went to funerals every day of their lives. I can hardly believe that my mother is related to them. The Sugdens refused a drink and had a cup of tea whilst my mother defrosted the turkey in the bath. I helped my father carry Queenie (fifteen stone) and Bert (fourteen stone) out of our car. Queenie is one of those loud types of old ladies who dye their hair and try to look young. Bert is in love with her. He told me when I was helping him into the toilet.

Grandma Mole and Auntie Susan came at twelve-thirty and pretended to like the Sugdens. Auntie Susan told some amusing stories about life in prison but nobody but me and my father and Bert and Queenie laughed.

I went up to the bathroom and found my mother crying and running the turkey under the hot tap. She said, "The bloody thing won't thaw out, Adrian. What am I going to do?" I said, "Just bung it in the oven". So she did.

We sat down to eat Christmas dinner four hours late. By then my father was too drunk to eat anything. The Sugdens enjoyed the Queen's Christmas message but nothing else seemed to please them. Grandma Sugden gave me a book called *Bible Stories for Boys*. I could hardly tell her that I had lost my faith, so I said thank you and wore a false smile for so long that it hurt.

The Sugdens went to their camp beds at ten o'clock. Bert, Queenie, and my mother and father played cards while I polished my bike. We all had a good time making jokes about the Sugdens. Then my father drove Bert and Queenie back to the home and I phoned Pandora up and told her that I loved her more than life itself.

I am going round to her house tomorrow to give her the deodorant and escort her to the pantomime.

Saturday, December 26th

BANK HOLIDAY IN UK AND REP. OF IRELAND (a day may be given in lieu) NEW MOON
The Sugdens got up at *7 am* and sat around in their best clothes looking respectable. I went out on my bike. When I got back my mother was still in bed, and my father was arguing with Grandad Sugden about our dog's behaviour, so I went for another ride.

I called in on Grandma Mole, ate four mince pies, then rode back home. I got up to 30 mph on the dual carriageway, it was dead good. I put my new suede jacket and corduroy trousers on (courtesy of my father's Barclaycard) and called for Pandora. She gave me a bottle of after-shave for my Christmas present. It was a proud moment, it signified the *End of Childhood*.

J cloth – *(brand name) cloth for cleaning dishes* ***Woodbines*** – *(brand name) cheap cigarettes* ***Bob Martin*** – *(brand name) dog food* ***Maltesers*** – *(brand name) chocolates* ***Dumbo*** – *(sl) stupid* ***tension*** – Spannung ***backstage*** – hinter der Bühne ***Close Encounters*** – *1977 science fiction film* ***break a leg*** *(theatre sl) good luck* ***to hiss*** – auszischen ***to waste*** – verschwenden ***hypocritical*** – heuchlerisch ***Nativity play*** – Krippenspiel ***mugged*** – *robbed on the street* ***dead*** – *(sl) completely* ***appreciative*** – *thankful*, ***wept***, *past of to weep – to cry* ***revelry*** – *wild and noisy celebrations* ***quid*** – *(GB sl) pound* ***hurt*** – beleidigt ***malicious*** – boshaft ***engaged*** – verlobt ***to cough up*** – *(sl) to give* ***conscience*** – Gewissen ***to the tune of*** – in Höhe von ***pantomime*** – *play with music and dancing based on a fairy story and performed at Christmastime in Britain* ***Boxing Day*** – *Dec 26* ***Cadbury's*** – *(brand name) chocolate* ***hangover*** – „Kater" ***row*** – Argument ***funeral*** – Beerdigung ***to defrost*** – auftauen ***stone*** – (BE) *14 pounds* ***to pretend*** – tun, als ob ***Queen's Christmas message*** – *shown on TV every Dec 25 at 3 pm* ***30 mph*** = *30 miles per hour* (ca. 48 km) ***dual carriage way*** – (BE) Schnellstraße ***suede*** – Wildleder

Christmas Dinner

turkey
sage and onion stuffing
gravy
*
roast potatoes
*
Brussels sprouts
*
Christmas pudding
with
brandy butter
*
mince pies

W	A	G	B	I	M	E	V	H	I	C
R	O	N	I	O	N	W	D	B	G	E
G	N	I	F	F	U	T	S	T	N	G
E	Y	D	N	A	R	B	H	U	Y	A
S	D	D	C	S	T	U	O	R	P	S
F	F	U	Q	G	P	K	J	K	O	E
X	L	P	O	T	A	T	O	E	S	I
K	Z	U	A	G	R	A	V	Y	T	P

Which words from the menu can you find in the tray?

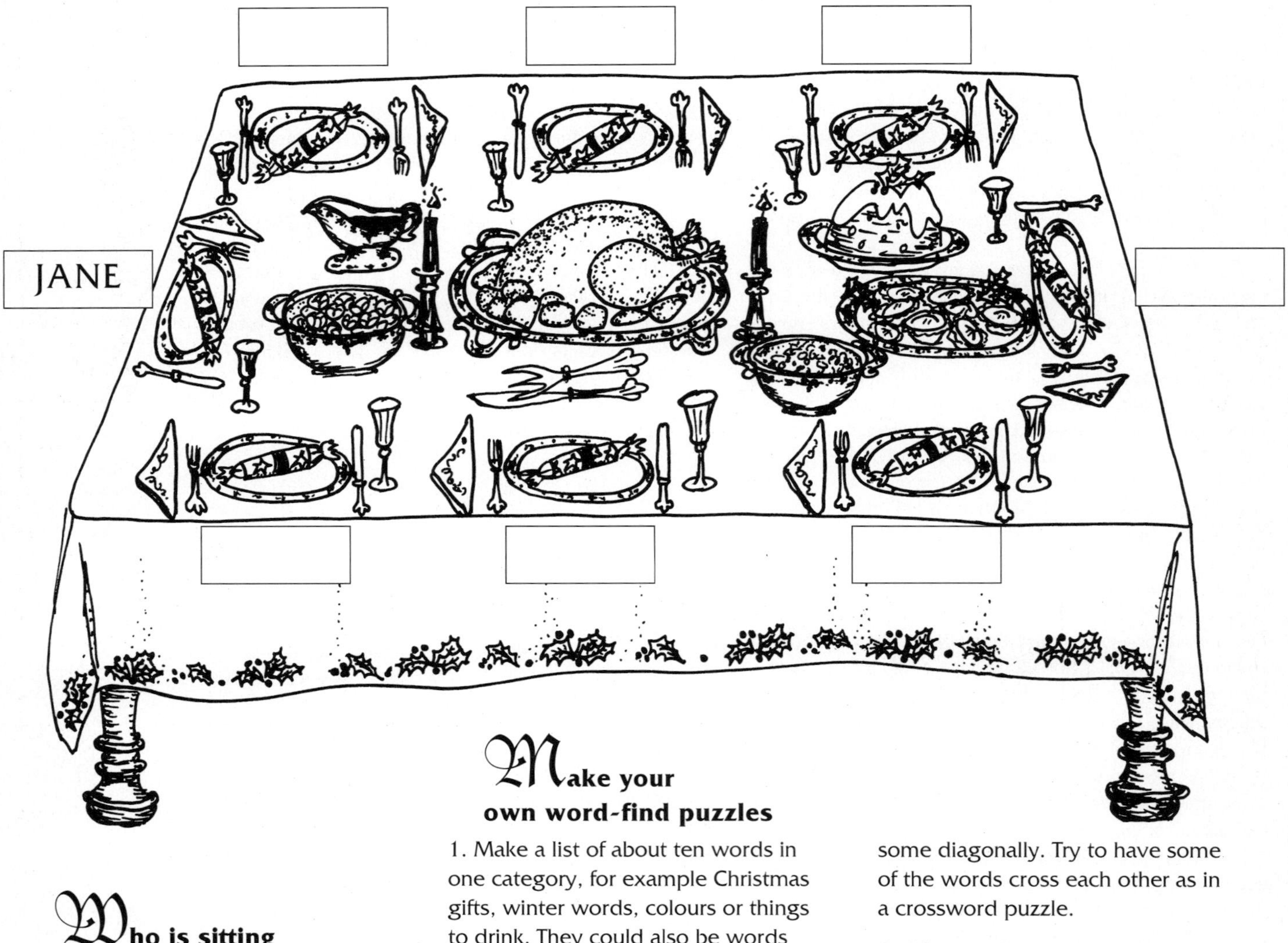

Who is sitting where at the Christmas table?

Julie is sitting next to Jack. James is sitting between Jason and Jill. Jack is on Jane's left. Jenny is opposite James. Jill is on John's right. Jason is sitting opposite Jane.

Make your own word-find puzzles

1. Make a list of about ten words in one category, for example Christmas gifts, winter words, colours or things to drink. They could also be words from a song, poem or story.

2. Write your words on a piece of graph paper (paper with little squares), putting one letter in each box.

3. Write some words across, some backwards, some going down and some going up. You can also write some diagonally. Try to have some of the words cross each other as in a crossword puzzle.

4. After you have written all your words, fill in the empty squares with any letters.

5. Photocopy your puzzle and your list of words and see how fast your friends can find the words. It's more difficult if you don't give them your word list, but only the category.

Christmas is TOGETHER Time

by Charles M. Schulz

1

2

3

4

5

6

7

8

9

10

11

12

Cut out the "Christmas is ..." sentences and match them to the pictures.

A Christmas is catching snowflakes.	**B** Christmas is cutting down your very own Christmas tree.	**C** Christmas is getting together with your family.
D Christmas is a time for miracles.	**E** Christmas is when your mailbox is so full that it doesn't echo.	**F** Christmas is when you get things you never really wanted.
G Christmas is a bad time to be away from home.	**H** Christmas is together time.	**I** Christmas is finding just the right place for the tree.
J Christmas is deciding who to include on your gift list.	**K** Christmas is a long, quiet nap after a long, delicious dinner.	**L** Christmas is a time of waiting ... and waiting ... and waiting ...

Under the Mistletoe

Mistletoe

Highly valued by both the Druids and the Norsemen, the mistletoe is surrounded by myth and legend. Most valued when growing on an oak, it had to be cut left-handed with a golden sickle by a fasting Druid clothed in a white tunic. And not only that, for if its ability to promote fertility and keep away witches was to be preserved, the mistletoe was not to be touched by iron or allowed to fall to the ground.

No one knows who first started the tradition of kissing under the mistletoe. It may have something to do with its alleged fertility powers or with the old custom of warriors declaring a truce whenever they met under a tree with mistletoe. In the old days, after each kiss a berry was plucked and when all the berries were gone, the mistletoe no longer had its magic power.

Mistletoe (Viscum album) *is a parasite that grows in other plants. The fact that it doesn't have direct contact with the ground but hangs mysteriously between the earth and the sky is one reason ancient people found it so magical. In England, mistletoe is most abundant on apple trees, more rarely on oaks. Birds eat the berries and spread the seeds through their droppings. A sticky substance from the berries also sticks to the birds' beaks. When they try to rub it off on the bark of a tree, they also spread the mistletoe seeds.*

MISTLETOE

Sitting under the mistletoe
(Pale-green, fairy mistletoe),
One last candle burning low
All the sleepy dancers gone,
Just one candle burning on,
Shadows lurking everywhere:
Some one came, and kissed me there.

Tired I was: my head would go
Nodding under the mistletoe
(Pale-green, fairy mistletoe),
No footsteps came, no voice, but only,
Just as I sat there, sleepy, lonely,
Stooped in the still and shadowy air
Lips unseen – and kissed me there.

Walter de la Mare

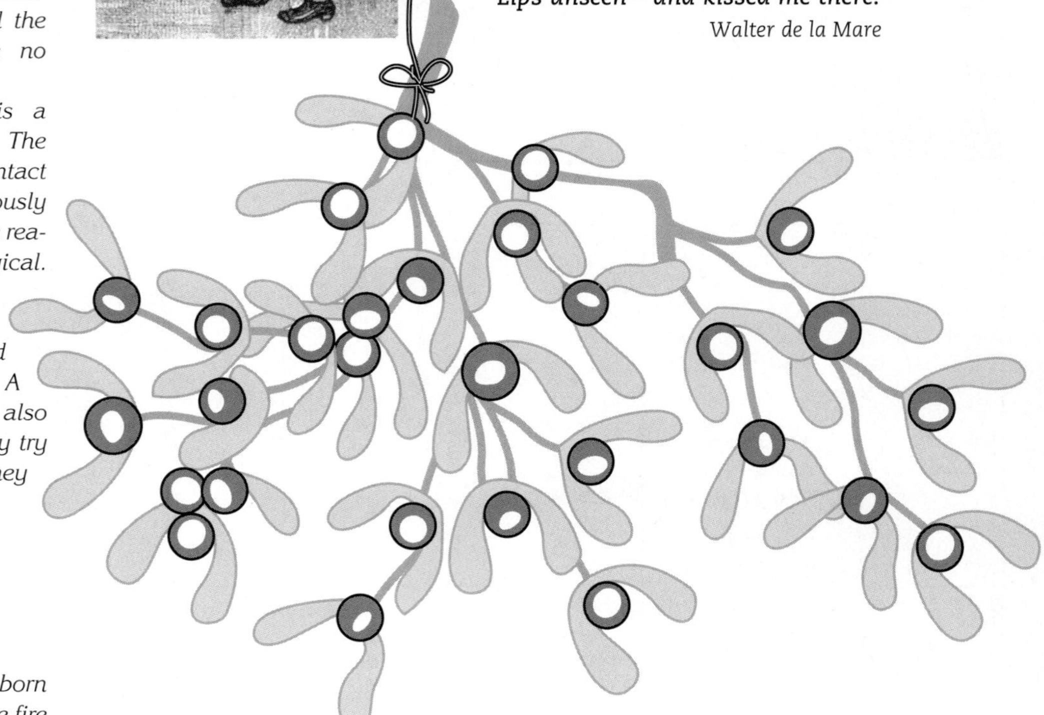

Robin Redbreast

It is said that after Jesus was born Joseph went out to gather fuel for the fire and was gone so long that Mary became anxious that the fire would go out. Suddenly some small brown birds flew in and began to fan the fire with their wings, keeping it alight until Joseph returned.

But Mary saw that they had scorched their breasts and said, "From now on you will always have a fiery red breast in memory of what you have done for the baby Jesus. People will love you and will call you Robin Redbreast."

THE ROBIN

Art thou the bird whom man loves best,
The pious bird with the scarlet breast,
Our little English robin;
The bird that comes about our doors
When autumn winds are sobbing?
The bird who by some name or other
All men who know thee call their brother?

William Wordsworth

The Chime Child

by Ian Strachan
(Abridged)

I've never believed in ghosts. To me they're as unlikely as snow on Christmas Day. But what happened to a young friend of mine last year has left me wondering.

Tired of all the commercialization of Christmas, her father had decided that they should have a totally different kind of celebration and had rented *The Old Parsonage* for them to stay in, buried deep in the Suffolk countryside. My friend Christy, due to celebrate her thirteenth birthday that particular Christmas Day, thought it was a boring idea and would much rather have spent time with her friends. But two nights before Christmas her parents stuffed the car with everything, including Christy's seven-year-old sister Emily, their dog Sam, a Christmas tree and loads of presents. Of course they should have known better than to set out when heavy snow began to fall even before they'd left London. But Dad would not turn back.

At last they arrived, exhausted, in a howling blizzard outside a big old house, already buried up to its window-sills in snow. When Mum tried to put the lights on, nothing happened. "The wind must have brought down the power cables," Dad said. Mum sighed, "That means there's no heat either, and unless we can get that old stove going, we can't even boil a kettle for a hot drink."

* * *

The next morning somebody banged heavily on the back door. Dad returned with an absolute mountain of a woman.

"I'm Mrs Pargeter," she announced in a loud voice. "I look after this place. I just popped over to see you'd got here safely and to bring you a few things I thought you might need."

She unloaded six bottles of milk, a dozen eggs and three loaves of bread.

"That's very kind of you," Mum said, "but to be honest we were thinking of going home again."

"You'll not make it!" Mrs Pargeter said bluntly. "It'll be days before the snowplough comes round here."

As Mum walked with Mrs Pargeter to the door, she asked her, "Will you come again tomorrow?"

Christy thought Mrs Pargeter looked slightly uncomfortable. "Christmas Eve? No, I'll not set foot in here again till Christmas is over. Mind you, I might see you at the late-night Christmas Eve service. You do go to church, don't you?" "Oh, yes," Mum lied.

"Could be rather nice, that," Dad said thoughtfully, "a midnight carol service."

* * *

Mum's thoughts had already turned to making a shopping list, and half an hour later Christy and her dad set out. Dad went to the supermarket, and Christy to the ironmonger's.

"Morning," said a tiny, bird-like man in the shop, "You'll be staying at the Old Parsonage."

"Well, yes."

"Plenty of people stay there in the summer, but I reckon you'll be the first to stay over Christmas."

The man leant over the counter and whispered, "It's only a story, but they do say a little girl was hidden away somewhere in that house by her wicked uncle and left to die a slow, terrible death."

Christy shivered. "Ugh! How horrible."

"I suppose you haven't heard anything unusual up there? Noises or anything?"

"You don't mean there's a ghost?"

"I don't suppose you believe in ghosts?"

"No, of course not," Christy said firmly. "Oh, one more thing. Have you got any birthday cake candles? Christmas Day's my birthday, just."

"What do you mean 'just'?"

"Mum thought I was going to happen on Christmas Eve, but I was born on the last stroke of midnight. That's why they called me Christy."

"The last stroke of midnight," the man said thoughtfully. "Then you're what's known round here as a Chime Child. You know, anyone born while the clock is chiming at midnight has special powers. Those born at midnight are said to be able to see ghosts and talk to them."

* * *

The family went to bed early that night.

Christy awoke by the sound of Sam howling. She lit a candle and went downstairs. It was as she was passing the stone wall on her way back to bed that she heard the child sobbing. At first she thought it must be Emily, but her sister was upstairs and this sounded much closer.

"Who's there?" she asked quietly, holding the candle with a shaking hand.

Silence. "Who IS that?" There was a short pause, but no reply, and then the sobbing started again.

Now she knew where it came from. It was as if somebody was behind the oak chest at the base of the stone wall.

"Why are you doing this to me?" Christy asked desperately. She stood waiting, by now shivering with cold and fear, but nothing else happened.

* * *

The next afternoon, the storm outside was growing even fiercer. Christy went up to her bedroom to finish some last-minute present-wrapping. There, on a shelf of dusty books, she noticed an old local guide-book.

In it she found:

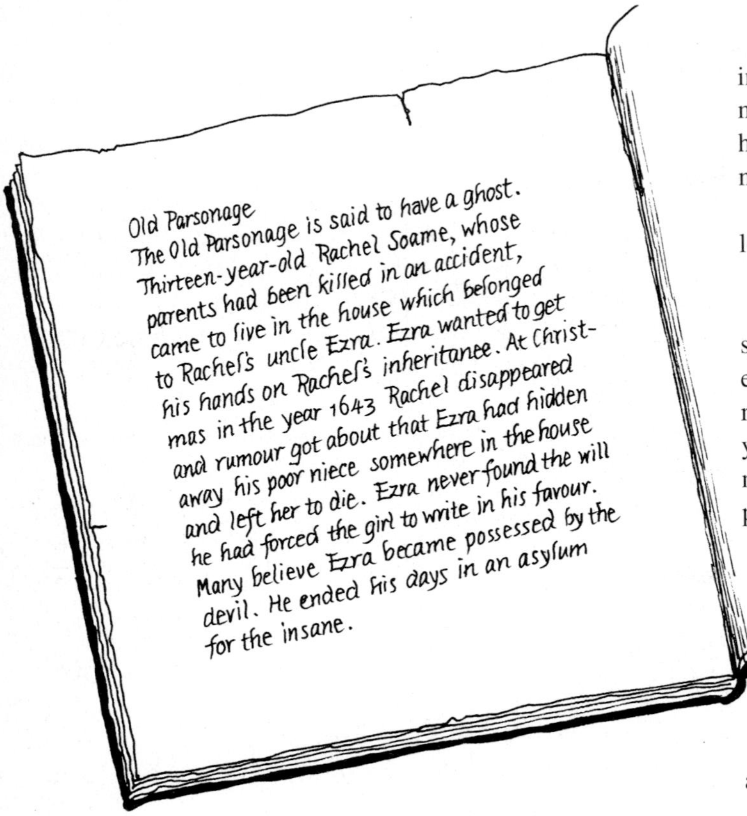

* * *

Late in the evening the whole family set out for the carol service. The church was beautifully decorated and, for the first time since they'd arrived in the village, Christy felt comfortable. She enjoyed singing the familiar carols and hearing the clock above them strike midnight.

After the service, as Christy was closing the gate of the churchyard, she noticed a figure in the shadow. She drew back, but his voice was comforting. "Don't be afraid, I'm only here to offer help."

"Who are you?"

"One of the Ancient Order of the Druids." Moonlight through the clouds revealed a tall figure dressed in long flowing robes with a hood which hid his face. He stretched out a hand towards her. When he opened it Christy jumped, for a knife lay in his hand. The Druid said quietly, "Take it."

Christy obeyed. "Is it gold?"

The figure nodded. "Remember, to retain the power, cut only with this."

"Cut what? What power? What are you talking about?"

But when she looked up, the figure had disappeared. "Come on, Christy, we're all waiting," her father called. She hurriedly put the knife into her pocket and ran to catch up. "Happy birthday, darling!" Mum said, giving her a big hug.

Back at the house, Mum made them all hot drinks, and they hung up their stockings for Father Christmas to fill during the night.

* * *

A deep slow rumble followed by a loud crash woke Christy. Lighting her candle, she quickly made her way downstairs.

In the corridor she saw that the stone wall had collapsed completely, burying the oak chest. She opened a door. There, inside, was a girl of Christy's age. She wore a plain white nightdress and her arms and legs were painfully thin. Her black hair emphasized the deathly whiteness of her skin. There was no doubt in Christy's mind that this was Rachel Soame.

"Christy! I thought you were never coming. I've waited so long for your help."

"But what can I do?" Christy asked.

"You have been sent to use your special powers against the spirit of my uncle Ezra! I have always hidden and managed to escape him, but this year, knowing of your presence, I have risked coming out to confront him. If I am not to be destroyed, you must equip yourself. There is something special you need – mistletoe. Since the dawn of time it has had mystical powers of protection against evil."

"But there's none in the house," Christy replied.

"Collect a branch of it from the old oak tree near the road and bring it back to the house. Go now – there's not a second to lose!"

"I'm not sure I'll be able to find the tree in all the snow."

"Be led by your heart," Rachel said earnestly, "but above all be quick. He'll be here at four o'clock."

The icy wind was whipping up the powdery snow in blinding clouds. Christy stumbled several times, and then suddenly her leg sank into a drift and she fell forward. The next thing she remembered was awakening as if from a deep sleep. Christy faintly heard the three-quarter hour striking. Only fifteen minutes were left before Ezra would attack Rachel. Then she noticed something like a tiny pearl on her anorak. "A mistletoe berry!" She realized she must have fallen on the trunk of a fallen oak tree. Immediately she began digging through the snow, and at last she found some mistletoe. She grabbed a branch of it, but it refused to break. The Druid's words came back to her: "To retain the power, cut only with this." She took the knife and put the golden blade to the branch.

* * *

The house stood dark and totally silent. Perhaps she was already too late?

Rachel lay motionless on the floor. "I thought you were never coming. Uncle Ezra is near." "What do I do with the mistletoe now that I've got it?"

"First, cut a sprig for me to hold."

Christy did as she was told and Rachel clutched it in both hands on her chest. "Use the golden knife to put a sharp point on the end of the main branch. You must drive it into his heart."

Christy's hand shook with fear at the thought while she cut off the bark. She had just finished when she heard the roar of a man's voice.

Ezra stood in the doorway, a short fat man, dressed in faded black.

"Rachel!" he shouted. "Your time has come. This year I WILL take you back with me!"

Christy was shaking, but she managed to say, "No, you won't."

"Who are you? I warn you, leave my affairs alone."

He took a step towards Rachel.

Cornelsen

So this is Christmas and what have you done?

Keine Lust, selbst zu singen?

Dann probieren Sie's doch mal mit der *Merry Christmas* CD/CC!
Der Schülerchor der internationalen John F. Kennedy-Schule singt traditionelle und moderne Weihnachtslieder und bringt so weihnachtliche Stimmung in Ihr Klassenzimmer.

Außerdem kann man einer *Christmas ghost story* lauschen, ein ungewöhnliches Weihnachtsspiel verfolgen oder zuhören, wie der *Service of Nine Lessons and Carols* im King's College, Cambridge jedes Jahr beginnt.

Alles, was es auf der CD/CC zu hören gibt, ist im Heft markiert.

Bestellkarte

Hiermit bestelle ich zu den ausgewiesenen Abgabebedingungen:

☐ **Cassette zu Merry Christmas**
Laufzeit ca. 70 Minuten, Bestellnummer 67726 ◊ 29,80 DM

☐ **CD zu Merry Christmas**
Laufzeit ca. 70 Minuten, Bestellnummer 67734 ◊ 32,90 DM

Gewünschtes bitte in dem entsprechenden Kästchen deutlich ankreuzen. Die Cassetten können auch durch den Buchhandel bezogen werden. Preisstand 1.1.1997. Änderungen vorbehalten.
◊ = Unverbindliche Preisempfehlung.

Bitte in Druckschrift ausfüllen

Name / Vorname

Straße / Hausnummer

Postleitzahl / Ort

Ort / Datum

Unterschrift des / der Erziehungsberechtigten

Bitte freimachen

Antwortkarte

Cornelsen

Cornelsen Verlagskontor

33598 Bielefeld

"Don't touch her," Christy said quietly. "Leave her alone."

"If you will not listen to me, I must teach you a lesson."

With a sharp crackle, a flash of blue-green lightning burst from Ezra's finger-ends. Christy felt something like a hammer-blow hit her as she crashed backwards. Ezra gave a grim smile, but his expression changed when he bent over Rachel and saw the mistletoe she was clutching. Taking the long brass poker from the fireplace, he tried to knock the mistletoe from Rachel's hand, but the poker glowed white-hot and he dropped it with a howl.

"Come with me," Ezra said, dragging Christy towards Rachel.

"Take off that vile thing," he commanded. Christy was about to remove the sprig of mistletoe from Rachel's hands when she saw the bigger branch of it under the sofa. With enormous effort, she reached out for it. As she grasped the branch she felt warmth flowing back into her body.

"Don't think to threaten me," Ezra warned, but his face paled. He rushed at her and, without thinking, Christy hit him with the only thing she had – the mistletoe.

The branch caught him on the arm. There was a vivid golden flash, a smell of flesh burning, and Christy watched in horror as Ezra's arm sizzled and burned in his sleeve. He attempted to aim another flash of green lightning at her, but she hid behind her only shield, the mistletoe.

Realising the power she held, Christy began to go after him, making certain that she kept the branch between them. They circled the room, knocking over the Christmas tree and scattering presents. She was about to drive the sharp stick into his body when he snatched up a little stool. Lifting it high above his head, he brought it crashing down on Christy.

She staggered back, knocking over the oil lamp, and the spilt paraffin burst into flames. Too late, she realised that she had again lost the mistletoe.

"Aha! I have you," Ezra snarled. "Now we'll play this game my way."

The flames dancing around her, Christy grabbed the sprig from Rachel's hands. Then she remembered the golden knife, and while she threw the mistletoe at Ezra, she snatched it from her pocket.

The mistletoe caught him full in the face. He cried out in agony, staggered forward, tripped over and fell. He toppled towards her, Christy screaming in terror, and landed on the golden knife.

The body of Ezra Dexter crumbled away into powder, caught alight and burned with an intense heat until there was nothing left – nothing but the knife, twisted by the heat and bearing an ugly green stain on the blade. Rachel stood up. Colour was already flooding back into her cheeks. "Thank you," she said.

Then Christy realised the girl was slowly fading away.

* * *

Christy woke to find her mother bending over her. "Happy birthday, Christy. Thank you for getting up early to bring in some mistletoe, but you really shouldn't have left it lying on the floor." Christy glanced round the room. There was no sign of the fight, let alone a fire. Broken ornaments and disturbed furniture were all safely back in their original positions, and the presents were stacked neatly beneath the tree.

What had happened? Had *anything* happened, or had it all been some nightmare brought on by everything she had heard and read about the Old Parsonage? But then she remembered the mistletoe – that was real enough – and the knife? Slowly Christy unlocked her clenched fingers and raised her right hand. There it lay in her hand, twisted as if by intense heat, its blade marked by an ugly green stain.

She stood for a moment longer, gazing at the knife, then she smiled, put it in her pocket, and turned back to join her family in the joy of Christmas and the beginning of a new year in her life.

* * *

So now you may understand my uncertainties about the existence of ghosts, especially as, while I've been telling this extraordinary tale, the golden knife lies before me. But perhaps my doubts are only prompted by the owls hooting close to the house, the desolate barking of the foxes in the wood, and the grandfather clock, which is chiming midnight.

chime – *sound of bells* ***parsonage*** – Pfarrhaus ***mind you*** – allerdings ***ironmonger's*** – Eisenwarenhandlung ***to sob*** – schluchzen ***oak chest*** – Eichenkiste ***inheritance*** – Erbschaft ***rumour*** – Gerücht ***will*** – Testament ***insane*** – *crazy* ***drift*** – Schneewehe ***bark*** – Borke, Rinde ***vile*** – *extremely bad* ***to pale*** – *to become white* ***stool*** – Hocker ***agony*** – *extreme suffering* ***to fade away*** – *to disappear slowly* ***let alone*** – geschweige denn ***nightmare*** – *bad dream* ***extraordinary*** – *very unusual* ***tale*** – *story* ***to prompt*** – wecken ***owl*** – Eule

God Rest Ye Merry, Gentlemen

Words and tune English traditional

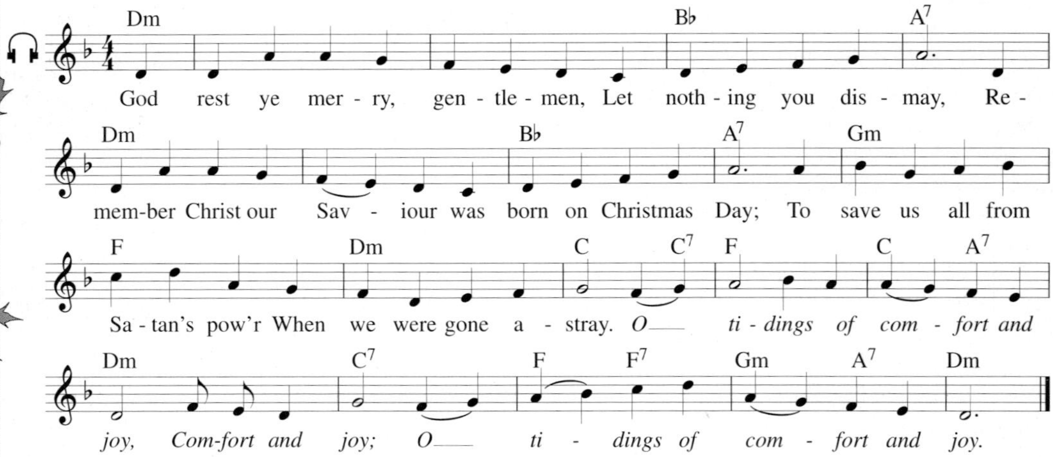

From God our heavenly Father
A blessed angel came;
And unto certain shepherds
Brought tidings of the same;
How that in Bethlehem was born
The Son of God by name,

Refrain

Deck the Hall

Welsh traditional

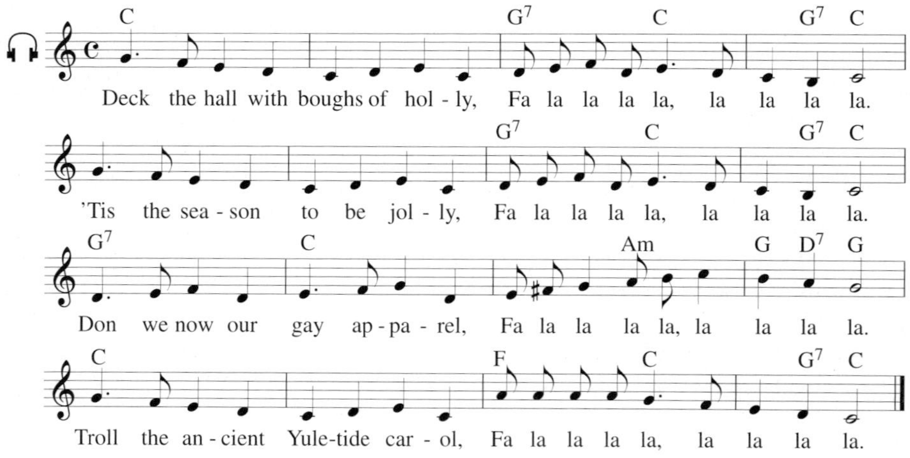

See the blazing Yule before us,
Fa la la la la, la la la la.
Strike the harp and join the chorus,
Fa la la la la, la la la la.
Follow me in merry measure,
Fa la la, la la la, la la la.
While I tell of Yuletide treasure,
Fa la la la la, la la la la.

Fast away the old year passes,
Fa la la la la, la la la la.
Hail the new, ye lads and lasses,
Fa la la la la, la la la la.
Sing we joyous all together
Fa la la, la la la, la la la.
Heedless of the wind and weather
Fa la la la la, la la la la.

THE STORY OF CHRISTMAS

Why do we hang up the holly, decorate a tree, steal a kiss under the mistletoe and give presents at Christmas? Colm Murray unwraps the Noel truth.

(Abridged)

This Christmas I think I shall spend the holiday in the "traditional" way. I shall drink too much, eat too much, and have a good old time. In church I will pay homage to the birth of Jesus Christ. I will enjoy the bright blaze in the hearth as I decorate the evergreen Christmas tree and hang up the holly and mistletoe.

Or perhaps I'll be really different and celebrate in the way our ancient ancestors did. That means I would drink too much, eat too much, and have a good old time. In homage to the sun, I could light many big fires and decorate my home with evergreens as a symbol of my faith in the regeneration of life. In short, I would defy the bleak winter and forget my troubles.

As you can see, many of the customs we associate with the festive season today have their roots in our dim, pagan past. These traditions have been carried from ancient Europe to the modern household and now are part of the festive season. Without them, it just wouldn't be the same.

There has always been a mid-winter festival in Europe. The northern Germanic tribes celebrated Yuletide (according to some sources on 22 December), while in southern Europe the Roman Empire had the Saturnalia, which began on 17 December. With great fires, bright lights, evergreen revelry, both traditions defied the bite of winter and encouraged the sun to return once again.

However, the early Christians looked upon these festivals with, I imagine, not a little envy. By the fourth century the Church had decided on 25 December as the date to celebrate the birth of Jesus Christ. It was easier than trying to force old habits out of the people.

For example, in Anglo-Saxon England, 25 December had been the traditional beginning of the New Year, and so the Church encouraged people to look on this time not as Yule but as a celebration of Christ's birth.

Festivities varied from country to country, but the one common aspect in all the traditions was that they each had their own spirits and "personifications" of the Christmas spirit.

Although the Santa Claus of today is a relatively recent phenomenon, his earliest manifestation was in the form of St Nicholas, who lived in the early fourth century and was Bishop of Myra in Lycia (now part of Turkey). Santa Claus rapidly swept aside other traditional contenders for his crown. By the mid-1800s the English Father Christmas and the American version of the Dutch "Sinterklaas" had become the same person.

It is the Victorian sentimental interpretation of the season that we have to thank for giving us many of the customs that we observe today. For example, the tree was introduced to England by German immigrants and became extremely popular following Queen Victoria's marriage in 1840 to Prince Albert of Saxe-Coburg-Gotha.

The kiss beneath the mistletoe is an English custom dating back to the early 17th century at least. Before the Christmas tree became popular, the centrepiece of English homes had been the "kissing branch". These were lit with candles stuck in apples and decorated with mistletoe. Yet when the Christmas tree replaced them, the Victorians kept mistletoe popular, enjoying the freedom it gave them to embrace members of the opposite sex in public without scandal!

The first Christmas card was almost certainly designed by H. C. Horseley in 1843. The custom became so popular that by the 1890s the Post Office was struggling with the seasonal explosion in its mail.

Again it was during this time that the traditional turkey dinner became popular. The Victorians felt their lifestyle was unsuited to the old excesses, and a turkey or goose replaced the traditional boar's head – and who can blame them?

Since 1900 the increase in the observance of Christmas has been enormous. Preparations begin earlier and earlier each year – there are even specialist "Christmas Shops" open all the year round for presents and decorations – and the holiday itself has become longer. The celebrations have become another multi-million pound industry. But, as you wade through the mire of commercialism, you might pause a while and perhaps raise a glass to all the rich beliefs and customs which have been blended together to make the occasion. It will help to prevent you tearing your hair out in rush and panic. But then again, I suppose the panic has become a custom in itself. Happy Christmas!

Charles Dickens's

A Christmas Carol

Mr. Fezziwig's Ball

Tiny Tim did NOT die. And there's good reason to believe that neither he, nor Ebenezer Scrooge, nor Bob Cratchit ever will.

Best-sellers come, best-sellers go. Few last as long as Charles Dickens's much-loved tale *A Christmas Carol*. Though written in 1843, it is still popular today, not only as a book, but in video and audio versions as well.

Dickens wrote *A Christmas Carol* in just six weeks, entering into the spirit of his own story so thoroughly that in writing it he wept and laughed and wept again. According to biographer Peter Ackroyd, he said Tiny Tim and Bob Cratchit were "ever tugging at his coat sleeve, as if impatient for him to get back to his desk and continue the story of their lives."

Artist John Leech, who was to become one of Dickens's closest friends, did the entrancing drawings for the first edition. Dickens persuaded his publisher to bind his little book in red and gold, with gilding on the edges of the pages. Published on 18 December 1843, it outsold other Christmas books by far.

Just 31 when he wrote *A Christmas Carol,* Dickens was already famous. On his trip to the United States the previous year, he had been mobbed by crowds eager to see the author of *The Pickwick Papers* (written when he was 25). Like *Pickwick* and Dickens's other books, *A Christmas Carol,* was pirated by American publishers and quickly became a hit on that side of the Atlantic, too. Peter Ackroyd reports that it so touched the heart of one American factory owner that he gave his workers an (unheard of) extra day's holiday.

A Christmas Carol began, and 15 years later ended, Dickens's famous public readings of his works. The demand for tickets for these dramatic performances – Dickens had once aspired to be an actor and all through his life engaged in amateur theatricals – was enormous. Both in England and on his triumphal tour of America after the Civil War, he read to packed houses.

Dickens's very last reading of *A Christmas Carol* in London, just a few months before his death, was followed by a "storm of cheering." That cheering – for Scrooge, for Tiny Tim, for the Dickensian vision of Christmas that prompted the saying he invented it – hasn't stopped yet, and the chances are it never will.

Scrooge and Bob Cratchit

to persuade – überreden ***publisher*** – Verleger ***to mob somebody*** – jemanden belagern ***cheering*** – Jubel ***Dickensian*** [– ' – – –] ***to prompt*** – hervorrufen ***saying*** – Spruch

EBENEZER SCROOGE

A play based on *A Christmas Carol*
by Charles Dickens
(Adapted by Kathleen Jalalpour)

SCENE ONE
Market Place - Sellers call "Fresh fish! Holly! Mistletoe! Hot soup! Apples!"

FRUIT SELLER Here comes that old miser Ebenezer Scrooge – He won't buy any of your holly or mistletoe, that's for sure!

FLOWER SELLER Nor any of your shiny apples, I dare say! No, it'll be the thin barley soup for Mr Scrooge, mark my words on that!

FISH SELLER He's so mean, it's awful. My cousin Bob Cratchit works for him, and Scrooge won't even heat up the place decently. And he was angry because Bob wanted to stay home with his family on Christmas - his only holiday of the year.

FRUIT SELLER I'd love to give him a lesson on what Christmas is really about, the old miser, that I would!

FLOWER SELLER Shhh here he comes!

SCROOGE A bowl of soup, and make it snappy, young man.

SOUP SELLER Yes, sir. Here you are, sir. That'll be ten pence, sir.

SCROOGE That's highway robbery! For a thin, tasteless soup such as this. Take your pence, then, thief!

SOUP SELLER Yes, sir, and Merry Christmas to you, Mr Scrooge.

SCROOGE Bah, humbug!

SCENE TWO
Scrooge sits in chair, eating.

MARLEY Ebenezer Scrooge! Eb-en-ez-er Scrooge!

SCROOGE What nonsense is this? Surely my eyes and ears deceive me! Marley – my old partner – it cannot be!

MARLEY It is I, Ebenezer. I return from the realm of the dead to give you an urgent warning. Change your ways, Ebenezer Scrooge. Change them or you will spend an eternity in misery as I do!

SCROOGE Be gone, ghost! I'm not afraid of you!

MARLEY You will be visited by three spirits. The first one will come at one o'clock tonight. Listen to them, Ebenezer Scrooge, and change your ways. It is your **last chance!**

Marley leaves. Scrooge sleeps. The clock strikes one.

SPIRIT OF CHRISTMAS PAST *sweetly* Awake, Ebenezer! Your past awaits you! *Ebenezer follows as in a dream.*

SCENE THREE
A young boy sits unhappily at a school desk alone.

PAST Do you recognize this lad, Mr Scrooge?

Scrooge nods sadly and points to himself. A girl enters the room.

SARAH Eb, come home now – it's all right. Father's better now. He won't hurt you. Come – the carriage is waiting.

EBENEZER Oh Sarah, it is nice to get away from boarding school. And I do miss you and Mother, but you know Father always gets angry with me – I can never do anything right.

SARAH Come now, Eb. Everything will be all right – it's almost Christmas!

Boy rises and leaves with sister.

PAST Do you remember being that boy, Mr Scrooge? Well, what about this young man, almost grown up?

Dancers enter, dance. Young man sits at table far away, writing numbers. Young woman enters, opens (imaginary) door, approaches him.

ISABEL Ebenezer. Why don't you come to the dance?

EBENEZER I must finish these accounts first.

ISABEL I need to talk to you about that, Ebenezer. You never have time for anything but your accounts and counting your money. What about me, Ebenezer? What about US?

EBENEZER What? Huh? Did you say something, Isabel?

ISABEL *Takes off ring, puts it on table.* Good-bye, Ebenezer.

She leaves. Ebenezer goes back to writing.

OLD SCROOGE No! No! You fool! Don't let her leave!

SCENE FOUR
The clock strikes two. Scrooge is in bed again. Spirit of Christmas Present enters.

PRESENT *loudly* Rise! Ebenezer Scrooge, follow me!

Spirit and Scrooge walk to a window. They see four people at a table.

SCROOGE Why, it's Bob Cratchit's family!

PRESENT Quiet, Ebenezer Scrooge! It is not a time for talking, but for listening!

MOTHER Come to the table, children. Father will be home soon. Bring your cups and we will have some tea.

LITTLE SISTER And then we'll have Christmas dinner with our giant roast goose.

BIG BROTHER It's not really such a big goose at all, if you ask me.

BIG SISTER Well, no one asked you, blockhead.

MOTHER Please don't fight, children. It's Christmas!

MR CRATCHIT Hello! I'm home!

BIG BROTHER Father – I bet that old miser Scrooge didn't give anyone a Christmas present this year, did he?

BIG SISTER He never does. He's the meanest man in London.

MR CRATCHIT Children, don't speak that way of your elders.

MOTHER Well, I'm sorry, Bob, but they're right. He's a cruel old miser, and you just put up with it. You never say a thing to him.

MR CRATCHIT Well, you know why I must put up with it. I'm lucky to have the job, and we need every penny to save up to get decent doctor care for our dear Tiny Tim.

LITTLE SISTER Oh, indeed, Father. I would give up ever so much if it would help cure Tiny Tim! Shh ... here he comes now!

Tim limps in.

TINY TIM Merry Christmas everyone! Isn't it wonderful that we're all together on this special day! I'm so lucky! None of the other lads have such a dear family to care for them. There's not a family in all of London that knows the true meaning of Christmas like this family does!

PRESENT *takes Scrooge back to bed.* Come, Ebenezer Scrooge!

SCROOGE *upset and worried.* Will the boy live, Spirit?

PRESENT Probably not, Ebenezer Scrooge, probably not. Cratchit doesn't earn enough money to pay for medicine and a good doctor for him.

SCENE FIVE
The clock strikes three. Spirit of future appears.

SCROOGE Ahhhhh!

FUTURE *Points only – three townspeople are standing near a gravestone talking.*

T1 Thank goodness he's dead, the mean old miser. I owe him money and now I needn't repay it!

T2 Me too! I must thank my lucky stars that he popped off when he did.

T3 I know it is wrong to speak poorly of the dead, but he never knew how to enjoy this world when he was in it.

T1 No – there was not one drop of human kindness in that old man!

T2 And there's not a single person in the whole world who misses him, now that he's gone!

T3 What's the use of a lot of money if you don't know how to really live, I ask you! *They leave.*

SCROOGE Who is this miserable creature they were talking about? *He pulls away branches to see the gravestone.* What! It's me!! Help me, God! I must prevent this. *Runs into the street, staggering.*

BOY Paper! Paper! Get your paper fresh off the press!

SCROOGE Boy, is that turkey in Mr Cooper's shop still there?

BOY You mean the giant one that's bigger than me?

SCROOGE Yes, exactly! Go get it and bring it to the Cratchits' house! *Gives him money.*

BOY But, that's too much money! *Scrooge smiles and waves to him.* It's for me? Thank you so much, sir, and Merry Christmas to you, sir.

SCROOGE *Whispers in a girl's ear.*

GIRL Yes sir, I know Dr Brown's home. Do you want me to send for the doctor for you, Mr Scrooge?

SCROOGE Yes, please tell Dr Brown I need to see him. But it's not for me, it's for Tiny Tim Cratchit.

GIRL Oh, that's wonderful, Mr Scrooge. Dr Brown is such a good doctor, I know he can cure Tiny Tim. Oh, that's ever so kind of you, Mr Scrooge.

SCROOGE Well, that's the spirit of Christmas, isn't it? What are we waiting for? Let's celebrate Christmas!

All rush on stage and sing "We Wish You a Merry Christmas."

miser – Geizhals ***barley*** – Gerste ***decently*** – anständig ***highway robbery*** – Straßenraub ***eternity*** – Ewigkeit ***to put up with something*** – sich etwas gefallen lassen ***to limp*** – humpeln ***to stagger*** – taumeln

CHARLES DICKENS
(1812–1870)

CHARLES DICKENS was England's most popular and successful writer of the 19th century. He lived in great style in a country house and his friends were the leading authors, artists and actors of the day.

But as a boy, his life was very hard. His family was so poor that they could not pay their debts and the father had to go to prison. When he was ten, Charles had to work in a factory to earn money for the family. His job was to put labels on bottles. When the family inherited some money, Charles was able to go to school for a few years, but he never went to college. He educated himself by reading and watching people.

Most of Dickens's writing is about the daily lives of poor people. He could describe scenes and characters so dramatically that his readers laughed and cried and enthusiastically waited for his next book. Three of his famous novels are *David Copperfield*, *Oliver Twist* and *A Tale of Two Cities*.

A Christmas Carol was an immediate success when it was first published in 1843 and it is still a Christmas classic. Even among people who have never read the book, the main character, Scrooge, is so well-known that his name has entered the language as a term for any mean miser. In English, Donald Duck's rich miserly uncle is called Scrooge McDuck.

O Come, All Ye Faithful

Tune J. F. Wade, 1711–86

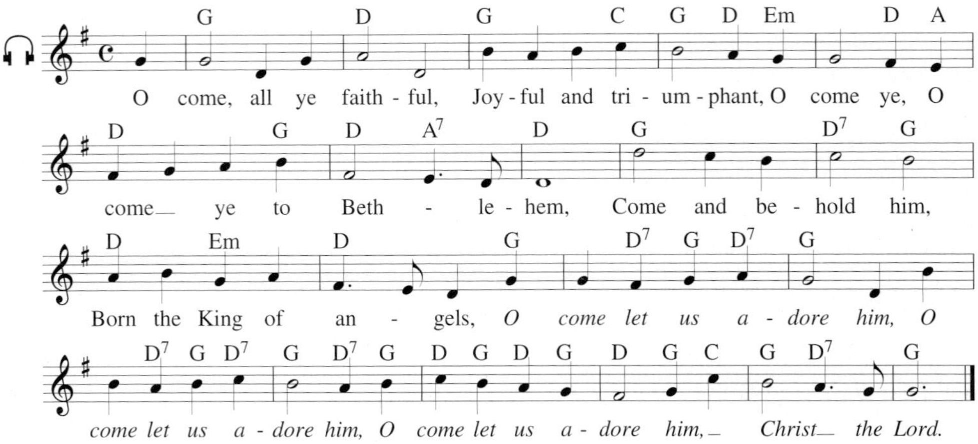

Sing, choirs of angels,
Sing in exultation,
O sing, all ye citizens of heaven above,
Glory to God all glory in the highest,

Refrain

The First Noel

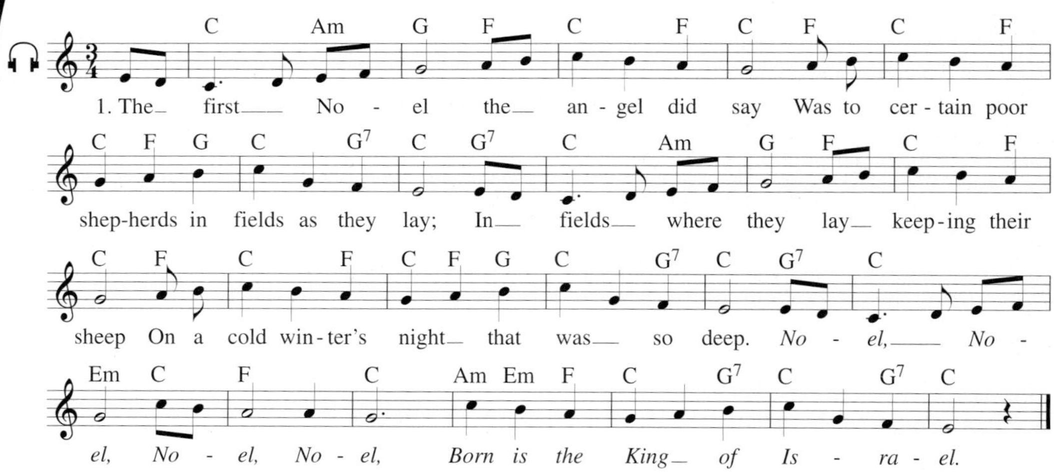

They lookèd up and saw a star,
Shining in the East, beyond them far,
And to the earth it gave great light,
And so it continued both day and night.

Refrain

And by the light of that same star
Three Wise Men came from country far.
To seek for a King was their intent,
And to follow the star wherever it went.

Refrain

This star drew nigh to the northwest
O'er Bethlehem it took its rest,
And there it did both stop and stay
Right over the place where Jesus lay.

Refrain

Then entered in those Wise Men three,
Fell reverently upon their knee,
And offered there, in His presence,
Their gold and myrrh and frankincense.

Refrain

THE CHRISTMAS SPIDER

by Marguerite de Angeli

THE grey spider worked very hard every day making long strands of silk that he wove into a web in which he caught troublesome flies. But he noticed that everyone turned away from him because, they said, he was so unpleasant to look at with his long, crooked legs and furry body. Of course the grey spider didn't believe that, because he had only the kindliest feelings for everybody. One day when he was crossing the stream he looked into the water. There he saw himself as he really was.

"Oh," he thought, "I *am* very unpleasant to look at. I shall keep out of people's way." He was very sad and hid himself in the darkest corner of the stable. There he again began to work as he always had, weaving long strands of silk into webs and catching flies. The donkey and the ox and the sheep that lived in the stable thanked him for his kindness, because now they were no longer bothered with the buzzing flies. That made the spider very happy.

One night, exactly at midnight, the spider was wakened by a brilliant light. He looked about and saw that the light came from the manger, where a tiny Child lay on the hay. The stable was filled with glory, and over the Child bent a beautiful mother. Behind her stood a man with a staff in his hand, and the ox and the donkey and all the white sheep were down on their knees.

Suddenly a gust of cold wind swept through the stable and the Baby began to weep from the cold. The mother bent over Him but could not cover Him enough to keep Him warm. The little spider took his silken web and laid it at Mary's feet (for it was Mary), and Mary took up the web and covered the Baby with it. It was soft as thistledown and as warm as wool. The Child stopped his crying and smiled at the little grey spider.

Then Mary said, "Little grey spider, for this great gift to the Babe you may have anything you wish."

"Most of all," said the spider, "I wish to be beautiful."

"That I cannot give you," Mary answered. "You must stay as you are for as long as you live. But this I grant you. Whenever anyone sees a spider at evening, he will count it a good omen, and it shall bring him good fortune."

This made the spider very happy, and to this day, on Christmas Eve, we cover the Christmas tree with "angel's hair" in memory of the grey spider and his silken web.

Spider's Web for the Christmas Tree

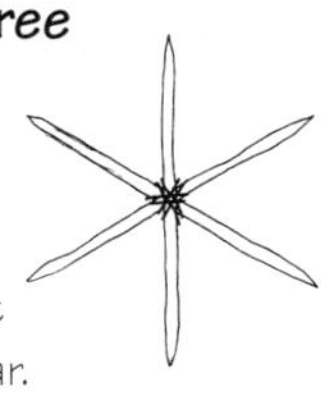

* Glue three cocktail sticks into a star shape. Take a piece of strong thread and tie it to the centre of the star. Wind it a couple of centimetres up to the first stick, wind it round twice, then move across to the next stick and wind it twice around that, and so on until you have completed one circle. Move the thread up another centimetre and make another circle in the same way, until gradually you have built up a web.

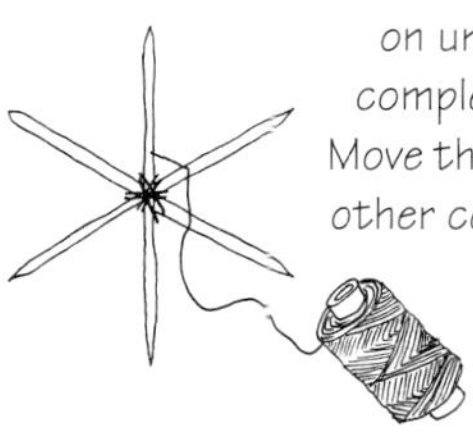

* Leave one long end of thread at the end to hang it from the tree. Spray the whole web with silver paint and dip in glitter to give it that added lustre of a real web.

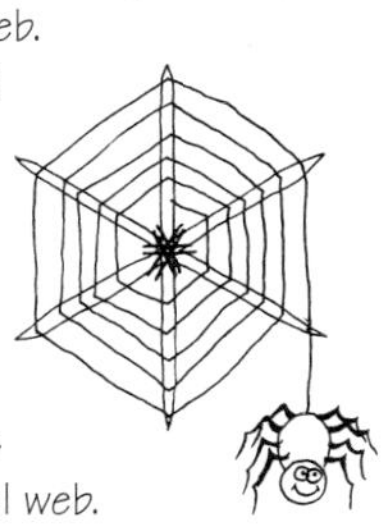

AWAY IN A MANGER

Words anon. (19th century American)
Tune A. Hume (1800–59)

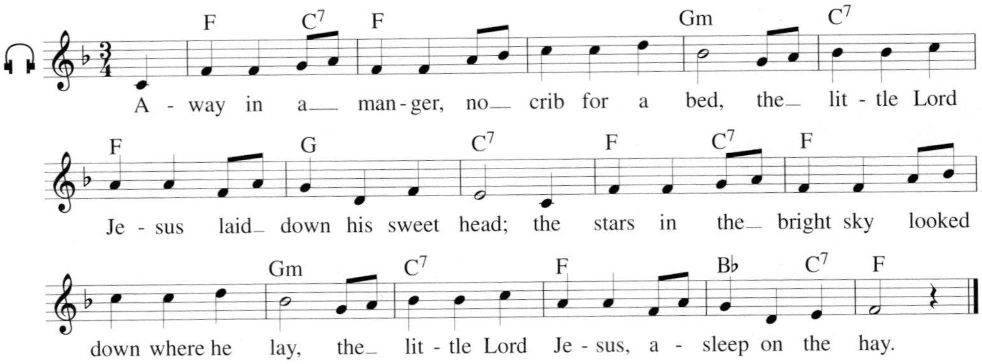

The cattle are lowing, the baby awakes,
But little Lord Jesus no crying he makes,
I love thee, Lord Jesus! Look down from the sky,
And stay by my side until morning is nigh.

WE THREE KINGS OF ORIENT ARE

Words and tune John H. Hopkins (1820–1891)

Born a King on Bethlehem's plain,
Gold I bring, to crown Him again,
King forever, ceasing never,
Over us all to reign.

Refrain

Christmas with the Herdmans

Based on the story "The Best Christmas Pageant Ever" by Barbara Robinson

The Herdmans were absolutely the worst kids in the history of the world. They lied and stole and smoked cigars (even the girls) and talked dirty and hit little kids.

Ralph, Imogene, Leroy, Claude, Ollie, and Gladys – six skinny, stringy-haired kids all alike except for being different sizes and having different black-and-blue places where they had clonked each other.

They lived over a garage at the bottom of Sproul Hill. Nobody used the garage any more, but the Herdmans used to bang the door up and down just as fast as they could and try to squash one another – that was their idea of a game.

Well, at the beginning of December it was time for the Sunday School children to start rehearsing for the Christmas pageant. But this year it was going to be different. My little brother Charlie had told the Herdmans that they gave away free candy and cake at church, so the Herdman kids all decided they wanted to be in the pageant. My mother was the director this year and when she asked who wanted to be Mary, Imogene Herdman was the only one who raised her hand.

IMOGENE I want to be Mary, and Ralph wants to be Joseph.

RALPH Yeah!

Mother just stared at them. It was like a detective movie, when the nice little old gray-haired lady sticks a gun in the bank window and says, "Give me all your money" and you can't believe it. Mother couldn't believe this.

Nobody volunteered to be Wise Men either, except Leroy, Claude and Ollie Herdman.

There was one Herdman left over, and one main role left over, and you didn't have to be very smart to figure out that Gladys was going to be the Angel of the Lord.

The first pageant rehearsal was usually about as much fun as a three-hour ride on the school bus, and just as noisy and crowded. This rehearsal, though, was different. Everybody shut up and settled down right away, for fear of missing something awful that the Herdmans might do.

They got there ten minutes late, sliding into the room like a bunch of outlaws about to shoot up a saloon. When Leroy passed Charlie he knuckled him behind the ear, and one little girl yelled as Gladys went by. But Mother had said she was going to ignore everything except blood, and since the kid wasn't bleeding, and neither was Charlie, nothing happened.

The Herdmans were the closest thing to criminals that we knew about, and they were going to represent the best and most beautiful. No wonder everybody was so worked up.

Mother started to separate everyone into angels and shepherds and guests at the inn, but right away she ran into trouble.

LEROY Who were the shepherds? Where did they come from?

RALPH What was the inn? What's an inn?

ALICE It's like a motel where people go to spend the night.

RALPH What people? Jesus?

The thing was, the Herdmans didn't know anything about the Christmas story. Mother said she had better begin by reading the whole story from the Bible.

MOTHER And Joseph with Mary, his espoused wife, being great with child …

RALPH Pregnant!

Well, that stirred things up. All the big kids began to giggle and all the little kids wanted to know what was so funny.

MOTHER That's enough, Ralph.

When Mother read about there being no room at the inn, Imogene's jaw dropped and she sat up in her seat.

IMOGENE My God! Not even for Jesus?

MOTHER Well, now, after all, nobody knew the baby was going to turn out to be Jesus.

RALPH You said Mary knew. Why didn't she tell them?

IMOGENE I would have told them! Boy, would I have told them! What was the matter with Joseph that he didn't tell them! Her pregnant and everything.

LEROY What was that they laid the baby in? That manger. Is that like a bed? Why would they have a bed in a barn?

MOTHER That's just the point. They *didn't* have a bed in the barn, so Mary and Joseph had to use whatever there was. What would you do if you had a new baby and no bed to put the baby in?

IMOGENE We put Gladys in a drawer.

MOTHER Well there you are. You didn't have a bed for Gladys so you had to use something else.

RALPH Oh we had a bed, only Ollie was still in it and he wouldn't get out. He didn't like Gladys. Remember how you didn't like Gladys?

MOTHER Anyway, Mary and Joseph used the manger. A manger is a large wooden feeding trough for animals.

IMOGENE You mean they put him in a feedbox? Where was the Child Welfare?

My mother just went on.

MOTHER And lo, the Angel of the Lord came upon them and the glory of the Lord shone round about them, and …

GLADYS Shazam!

MOTHER What?

GLADYS Out of the black night with horrible vengeance, the Mighty Marvo …

MOTHER I don't know what you're talking about, Gladys. This is the Angel of the Lord, who comes to the shepherds in the fields, and …

GLADYS Out of nowhere, right? In the black of night, right?

MOTHER Well, in a way.

So Gladys sat back down, looking very satisfied, as if this was at least one part of the Christmas story that made sense to her.

MOTHER Now when Jesus was born in Bethlehem of Judea, behold there came Wise Men from the East to Jerusalem, saying …

RALPH That's you, Leroy, and Claude and Ollie. So pay attention.

LEROY What does it mean, Wise Men? Were they like school teachers?

RALPH No dumbbell, it means like the President of the United States.

MOTHER *surprised and pleased* Why that's very close. Actually they were kings.

IMOGENE Well, it's about time. Maybe they'll tell the innkeeper where to get off, and get the baby out of the barn.

MOTHER They saw the young child with Mary, his mother, and fell down and worshipped him, and presented unto him gifts, gold and frankincense and myrrh.

LEROY What's that stuff?

MOTHER Precious oils and fragrant resins.

IMOGENE *yelling* Oil! What kind of a cheap king hands out oil for a present?

I couldn't understand the Herdmans. You would have thought the Christmas story came right out of the FBI files, they got so involved in it. They left the first rehearsal arguing about whether Joseph should have set fire to the inn, or just chased the innkeeper into the next county.

Since none of the Herdmans had ever gone to church, they didn't know how things were supposed to be. Imogene, for instance, didn't know that Mary was supposed to be acted out in one certain way – sort of quiet and dreamy and out of this world.

The way Imogene did it, Mary was a lot like Mrs Santoro at the Pizza Parlor. Mrs Santoro is a big fat lady with a little skinny husband and nine children, and she yells and hollers and hugs her kids and slaps them around.

That's how Imogene's Mary was – loud and bossy. She made the Wise Men keep their distance.

Finally the day of the pageant came and the church was crowded. First we sang "Away in a Manger," and then we were supposed to hum some more verses while Mary and Joseph came in from a side door. Only they didn't come right away. So we hummed and hummed and hummed, which is boring and also very hard, and before long doesn't sound like any song at all, more like an old refrigerator. Alice Wendlaken was pretty upset, as usual.

ALICE *loud whisper* I knew something like this would happen. They didn't come at all! We won't have any Mary and Joseph – and now what are we supposed to do?

I guess we would have gone on humming till we all turned blue, but we didn't have to. Ralph and Imogene were there all right, only for once they didn't come through the door pushing each other out of the way. They just stood there for a minute as if they weren't sure they were in the right place – because of the candles, I guess, and the church being full of people. I heard Alice gasp and she poked me.

ALICE I don't think it's very nice to burp the baby Jesus as if he had colic. Do you suppose he could have had colic?

I said I didn't know why not. He *could* have had colic, or been fussy. After all, that was the whole point of Jesus – that he didn't come down on a cloud like something out of "Amazing Comics" but that he was born and lived – a real person.

We had to sing extra loud when the shepherds came in because there were more shepherds than there were anything else, and they made so much noise, banging their crooks around like a lot of hockey sticks.

Next came Gladys, pushing people out of the way and stepping on everyone's feet. Since Gladys was the only one in the pageant who had anything to say, she made the most of it.

GLADYS Hey! Unto you a child is born!

She hollered as if it was, for sure, the best news in the world. And all the shepherds trembled, sore afraid – of Gladys, mainly, but it looked good anyway.

Then came all the angels. That took a long time because the little kids got nervous and cried and bent their wings in the door and things like that.

We got a little rest while the boys sang "We Three Kings of Orient Are" and everybody in the audience shifted around to watch the Wise Men march up the aisle.

ALICE *whispering* What have they got?

I didn't know, but whatever it was, it was heavy – Leroy almost dropped it. He didn't have his frankincense jar either, and Claude and Ollie didn't have anything, although they were supposed to bring the gold and the myrrh.

ALICE I knew this would happen. I bet it's something awful that they're bringing. – Like, like a burnt offering. You know the Herdmans.

Well, they did burn things, but they hadn't burned this yet. It was a ham – and right away I knew where it came from. My father was on the church charitable works committee – they give away food baskets at Christmas, and this was the Herdmans' food-basket ham. It still had the ribbons around it, saying Merry Christmas. The Herdmans had never before in their lives given anything away except lumps on the head. So you had to be impressed.

While we sang, the Wise Men were supposed to confer among themselves and then leave by a different door, so everyone would understand that they were going home another way, but the Herdmans forgot, or didn't want to, or something, because they didn't confer and they didn't leave either. They just sat there, and there wasn't anything anyone could do about it.

ALICE They're ruining the whole thing.

But they weren't at all. As a matter of fact, it made perfect sense for the Wise Men to sit down and rest, and I said so. They're supposed to have come a long way. You wouldn't expect them just to show up, hand over the ham, and leave.

As for ruining the whole thing, it seemed to me that the Herdmans had improved the pageant a lot, just by doing what came naturally – like burping the baby, for instance, or thinking a ham would make a better present than a lot of perfumed oil.

Usually by the time we got to "Silent Night", which was always the last carol, I was fed up with the whole thing and couldn't wait for it to be over. But I didn't feel that way this time. I almost wished for the pageant to go on, with the Herdmans in charge, to see what else they would do that was different.

When we got to the last verse of "Silent Night" I happened to look at Imogene and I almost dropped my song book on a baby angel. Everyone had been waiting all this time for the Herdmans to do something absolutely unexpected. And sure enough, that was what happened. Imogene Herdman was crying. In the candlelight her face was all shiny with tears and she didn't even bother to wipe them away.

* * *

Well, it *was* the best Christmas pageant we ever had. Everybody said so, but nobody seemed to know why.

As far as I'm concerned, Mary is always going to look a lot like Imogene Herdman – sort of nervous and bewildered, but ready to clobber anyone who laid a hand on her baby. And the Wise Men are always going to be Leroy and his brothers, bearing ham.

When we came out of the church that night it was cold and clear, with crunchy snow underfoot and bright, bright stars overhead. And I thought about the angel of the Lord – Gladys, with her skinny legs and her dirty sneakers sticking out from under her robe, yelling at all of us, everywhere:

GLADYS Hey! Unto you a child is born!

Christmas pageant – Krippenspiel ***skinny*** – *thin* ***to clonk*** – *to hit* ***rehearsal*** – Probe ***espoused*** – (*biblical*) anvertraut ***great with child*** – (*biblical*) schwanger ***jaw*** – Kiefer ***barn*** – Scheune ***drawer*** – Schublade ***welfare*** – Wohlfahrt ***shazam*** – *exclamation from comics: Wow!* ***vengeance*** – Rache ***where to get off*** – wo er sich hinscheren soll ***to gasp*** – nach Luft schnappen ***to burp*** – *to make a baby bring up air* ***colic*** – *stomach pain, in babies* ***fussy*** – quengelig ***sore*** – (*biblical*) *very* ***burnt offering*** – Brandopfer ***to confer*** [–ˈ–] *to discuss* ***as far as I'm concerned*** – was mich betrifft ***bewildered*** – *confused* ***to clobber*** – *to hit* ***sneakers*** – (AE) Turnschuhe

THE CHRISTMAS STORY

ACCORDING TO SAINT LUKE

And it came to pass in those days, that there went out a decree from Caesar Augustus, that all the world should be taxed.

(And this taxing was first made when Cyrenius was governor of Syria.)

And all went to be taxed, every one into his own city.

And Joseph also went up from Galilee, out of the city of Nazareth, into Judea, unto the city of David, which is called Bethlehem; (because he was of the house and lineage of David:)

To be taxed with Mary his espoused wife, being great with child.

And so it was, that, while they were there, the days were accomplished that she should be delivered.

And she brought forth her firstborn son, and wrapped him in swaddling clothes, and laid him in a manger; because there was no room for them in the inn.

And there were in the same country shepherds abiding in the field, keeping watch over their flock by night.

And, lo, the angel of the Lord came upon them, and the glory of the Lord shone round about them: and they were sore afraid.

And the angel said unto them, Fear not, for behold, I bring you good tidings of great joy, which shall be to all people.

For unto you is born this day in the city of David a Saviour, which is Christ the Lord.

And this shall be a sign unto you; Ye shall find the babe wrapped in swaddling clothes, lying in a manger.

And suddenly there was with the angel a multitude of the heavenly host praising God, and saying,

Glory to God in the highest, and on earth peace, good will toward men.

King James Bible, Authorized Version 1611

In those days a decree was issued by the emperor Augustus for a census to be taken throughout the Roman world.

This was the first registration of its kind; it took place when Quirinius was governor of Syria. Everyone made his way to his own town to be registered. Joseph went up to Judaea from the town of Nazareth in Galilee, to register in the city of David called Bethlehem, because he was of the house of David by descent; and with him went Mary, his betrothed, who was expecting her child. While they were there the time came for her to have her baby, and she gave birth to a son, her firstborn. She wrapped him in swaddling clothes, and laid him in a manger, because there was no room for them at the inn.

Now in this same district there were shepherds out in the fields, keeping watch through the night over their flock. Suddenly an angel of the Lord appeared to them, and the glory of the Lord shone round them. They were terrified, but the angel said, "Do not be afraid; I bring you good news, news of great joy for the whole nation. Today there has been born to you in the city of David a deliverer – the Messiah, the Lord. This will be the sign for you: you will find a baby wrapped in swaddling clothes, and lying in a manger. All at once there was with the angel a great company of the heavenly host, singing praise to God:

"Glory to God in highest heaven, and on earth peace to all in whom he delights".

The Revised English Bible 1989

ONCE IN ROYAL DAVID'S CITY

Words C.F. Alexander (1823–1895)
Tune H.J. Gauntlett (1805–1876)

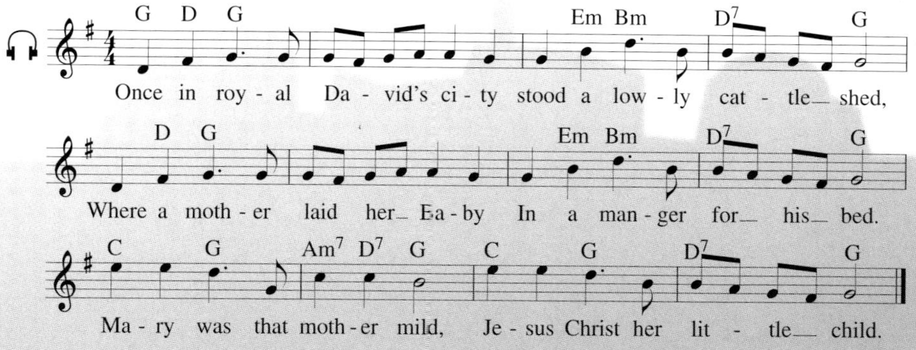

He came down to earth from heaven,
Who is God and Lord of all,
And his shelter was a stable,
And his cradle was a stall.
With the poor and mean and lowly,
Lived on earth our Saviour holy.

And through all his wondrous childhood
He would honour and obey,
Love and watch the lowly maiden
In whose gentle arms he lay.
Christian children all must be
Mild, obedient, good as he.

Every Christmas Eve since 1930 the BBC has broadcast the "Service of Nine Lessons and Carols" from King's College Chapel in Cambridge, England. When the young choir boys sing the carols, they know that millions of people around the world will be listening. One of the boys always starts the service by singing the first verse of "Once in Royal David's City", but the boys don't know who will have to sing the solo until just before the service begins!

MESSAGE TO THE SHEPHERDS

_ _ _ _ _ _ _ _ _ _ _ _ _ _ _ _ _

GO TELL IT ON THE MOUNTAIN

Christmas Spiritual

Down in a lowly manger,
Our humble Christ was born,
And God sent us salvation
That blessed Christmas morn.

AFRAID
ANGEL
BABY
BETHLEHEM
FIELDS
HEAVEN
JESUS
JOSEPH
LIGHT
MANGER
MARY
PEACE
SHEEP
SHEPHERDS
SING

The angels brought the shepherds good news of ___ ___ ___ ___ ___ ___ ___ ___
1 2 3 4 5 6 7 8

RUDOLPH THE RED-NOSED REINDEER

Words and music by Johnny Marks, 1949

And that's how Rudolph made history.

RUDOLPH AND I WERE SOMETHING ALIKE

by Robert L. May

The man who created the most famous reindeer of all tells why he did it.

An icy January blast tore at my coat as I hurried across the Chicago River bridge on my way to work. I noticed that the Christmas street decorations had been taken down, and in a way I was relieved. My wife was suffering from a long illness and I didn't feel very festive.

I was glad to get inside the foyer of the Montgomery Ward building. In the elevator I leaned back and listened to the younger men eagerly discuss their work.

"And how are you starting the new year?" I glumly asked myself. Here I was, heavily in debt at age 35 still grinding out catalogue copy. Instead of writing the great American novel, as I'd once hoped, I was describing men's white shirts.

It seemed I'd always been a loser. As a child I'd always been the smallest in the class. I was never asked to join the school teams. After mustering enough courage to ask a girl to dance, I'd catch her winking over my shoulder at a taller boy to get him to cut in.

As the elevator doors opened at my floor, I shrugged off my despondency. I had much to be thankful for. Despite my wife's grave illness, we had had many good years together. We also had four-year-old Barbara. God had been good to us.

In the copy department a secretary called, "Bob, the boss wants to see you."

What now? I wondered.

Our department head stood at the window in his office chewing his ever-present cigar. "Bob," he barked, "I've got an idea. For years our stores have been buying those little Christmas give-away coloring books from local peddlers. I think we can save a lot of money if we create one ourselves. You're pretty good at writing those song parodies for our company Christmas parties. Could you come up with a better booklet we could use?"

I started to answer but he kept right on talking. "I think it should be an animal story, with a main character like Ferdinand the Bull."

Finally I said I'd try. That night as I hung onto the strap in the lurching elevated train, I wondered about what kind of animal it should be. Christmas. Santa. Reindeer? Of course; it must be a reindeer! Barbara loved the deer down at the zoo.

I started puzzling over the plot. It should have a triumphant ending, tied to an unhappy beginning. And, of course, it must carry a lesson. But what could a little reindeer teach children? Suppose he were an underdog – a loser, yet triumphant in the end. Certainly a reindeer's dream would be to pull Santa's sleigh. But what could this one provide that Donner, Blitzen and the rest couldn't do?

Outside, the fog swirled in from Lake Michigan, dimming the street lights. Light. Something to help Santa find his way on a night like this. That was it! A reindeer with eyes like a cat. But ... then he would not be handicapped or an underdog. He'd be a super-deer.

Suddenly I had it! A nose. A bright red nose that would shine through fog like a floodlight. Quickly I worked up a rough plot about a little reindeer burdened with such a nose, a nose that other reindeer laughed at, but a nose that would help Santa bring joy to others.

The next morning I enthusiastically presented my idea to the boss. "For gosh sakes, Bob, can't you do better than that?" He clapped his hands over his eyes. "A red-nosed reindeer would be a monstrosity!"

I retreated to my desk and sat staring at the wall. I had faith in the reindeer I had by now named Rudolph. But how could I convince the boss?

An idea struck me. I walked over to the art department, where my friend Denver Gillen worked. "Denver, could you draw a deer with a big red nose and still make him look appealing?"

The following Saturday morning, Barbara, Denver and I met at the deer corral at Chicago's Lincoln Park Zoo and Denver began to sketch.

On Monday morning we brought the sketches into the boss's office. Slowly a smile crossed his face. "Bob," he said softly, "forget what I said and put the story into finished form."

I started writing. When I had got a few lines down I would call Barbara and her friends and read it aloud to them. If it held their attention I knew I was on the right track.

Spring slipped into summer. My wife's condition grew worse. Then in July she was gone.

At the office the boss put his hand on my shoulder. "Bob," he said, his voice unusually gentle, "I can understand your not wanting to go on with the kids' book. Give me what you've got and I'll let someone else finish it."

But I needed Rudolph now more than ever. Finally, in late August it was done. Rudolph was rushed into print and some 3,000,000 copies were given to children.

Ten years later, in 1949, Johnny Marks wrote the song "Rudolph the Red-Nosed Reindeer".

Today children all over the world read and hear about the little deer who started out in life as a loser, just as I did. But they learn that when he gave himself for others, his handicap became the very means through which he achieved happiness.

My reward is knowing that every year, when Christmas rolls around, Rudolph still brings that message to millions, both young and old.

One Foggy Christmas Eve ...

Poor Rudolph! He didn't know why the other reindeer always laughed at him.

One day he looked at his reflection in the water. He was shocked to see that his big red nose was so shiny that it glowed like a light.

The animals in the water and on the ice at the North Pole had never seen such a funny red nose. They all laughed at Rudolph.

Rudolph was very sad and he tried to hide his nose behind a tree. Santa Claus saw the light from behind the tree and knew that Rudolph was there.

"Well, hello Rudolph!" he said. "And Merry Christmas to you. I've brought you some food. But I'm afraid I have some sad news. It's so foggy tonight, I won't be able to bring any Christmas presents to the children this year."

Suddenly Santa had an idea. "Rudolph, could you help me tonight? Your shiny red nose can light the way for us!"

And so when Santa flew over the rooftops with a sleigh full of presents, Rudolph with his bright red nose was leading the way through the dark and foggy night.

The next day Rudolph was a hero. Now all the other reindeer wanted red noses, too. Rudolph was so happy that he gave each of his reindeer friends a Christmas gift – a shiny red nose.

HOW THE GRINCH

by Dr. Seuss

"And they're hanging their stockings!" he snarled with a sneer.
"Tomorrow is Christmas! It's practically here!"
Then he growled, with his Grinch fingers nervously drumming,
"I MUST find some way to stop Christmas from coming!"

For,
Tomorrow, he knew …
… All the *Who* girls and boys
Would wake bright and early. They'd rush for their toys!
And *then*! Oh, the noise! Oh, the Noise! Noise! Noise! Noise!
That's *one* thing he hated! The NOISE! NOISE! NOISE! NOISE!

Then the *Whos*, young and old, would sit down to a feast.
And they'd feast! *And they'd feast*!
And they'd FEAST!
FEAST!
FEAST!
FEAST!

Every *Who*
Down in *Who*-ville
Liked Christmas a lot …
But the Grinch,
Who lived just north of *Who*-ville,
Did NOT!

The Grinch *hated* Christmas! The whole Christmas season!
Now, please don't ask why. No one quite knows the reason.
It *could* be his head wasn't screwed on just right.
It *could* be, perhaps, that his shoes were too tight.
But I think that the most likely reason of all
May have been that his heart was two sizes too small.

But,
Whatever the reason,
His heart or his shoes,
He stood there on Christmas Eve, hating the *Whos*,
Staring down from his cave with a sour, Grinchy frown
At the warm lighted windows below in their town.
For he knew every *Who* down in *Who*-ville beneath
Was busy now, hanging a mistletoe wreath.

They would feast on *Who*-pudding, and rare *Who*-roast-beast
Which was something the Grinch couldn't stand in the least!

And THEN
They'd do something
He liked least of all!
Every *Who* down in *Who*-ville, the tall and the small,
Would stand close together, with Christmas bells ringing.
They'd stand hand-in-hand. And the *Whos* would start singing!
They'd sing! And they'd sing!
AND they'd SING! SING! SING! SING!
And the more the Grinch thought of this *Who*-Christmas-Sing,
The more the Grinch thought, "I must stop this whole thing!
"Why, for fifty-three years I've put up with it now!
"I MUST stop this Christmas from coming!
… *But HOW?*"

Then he got an idea!
An awful idea!
THE GRINCH
GOT A WONDERFUL, AWFUL IDEA!

STOLE CHRISTMAS!

"I know *just* what to do!" The Grinch laughed in his throat.
And he made a quick Santy Claus hat and a coat.
And he chuckled, and clucked, "What a great Grinchy trick!
With this coat and this hat, I look just like Saint Nick!"

"All I need is a reindeer ..."
The Grinch looked around.
But, since reindeer are scarce, there was none to be found.
Did this stop the old Grinch ...?
No! The Grinch simply said,
"If I can't *find* a reindeer, I'll *make* one instead!"
So he called his dog, Max. Then he took some red
thread
And he tied a big horn on the top of his head.

THEN
He loaded some bags
And some old empty sacks
On a ramshackle sleigh
And he hitched up old Max.
Then the Grinch said, "Giddap!"
And the sleigh started down
Toward the homes where the *Whos*
Lay a-snooze in their town.

All their windows were dark. Quiet snow filled the air.
All the *Whos* were all dreaming sweet dreams without care,
When he came to the first little house on the square.
"This is stop number one," the old Grinchy Claus hissed,
And he climbed to the roof, empty bags in his fist.

Then he slid down the chimney. A rather tight pinch.
But, if Santa could do it, then so could the Grinch.
He got stuck only once, for a moment or two.
Then he stuck his head out of the fireplace flue,
Where the little *Who* stockings all hung in a row.
"These stockings," he grinned,"are the *first* things to go!"

Then he slithered and slunk, with a smile most unpleasant,
Around the whole room, and he took every present!
Pop guns! And bicycles! Roller skates! Drums!
Checkerboards! Tricycles! Popcorn! And plums!
And he stuffed them in bags. Then the Grinch, very nimbly,
Stuffed all the bags, one by one, up the chimbley!

Then he slunk to the icebox. He took the *Whos'* feast!
He took the *Who*-pudding! He took the roast beast!
He cleaned out that icebox as quick as a flash.
Why, that Grinch even took their last can of *Who*-hash!

Then he stuffed all the food up the chimney with glee.
"And NOW!" grinned the Grinch, "I will stuff up the tree!"

And the Grinch grabbed the tree, and he started to shove
When he heard a small sound like the coo of a dove.
He turned around fast, and he saw a small *Who*!
Little Cindy-Lou *Who*, who was not more than two.

The Grinch had been caught by this tiny *Who* daughter,
Who'd got out of bed for a cup of cold water.
She stared at the Grinch and said, "Santy Claus, why,
"*Why* are you taking our Christmas tree? WHY?"

But, you know, that old Grinch was so smart and so slick
He thought up a lie, and he thought it up quick!
"Why, my sweet little tot," the fake Santy Claus lied,
"There's a light on this tree that won't light on one side.
"So I'm taking it home to my workshop, my dear.
"I'll fix it up *there*. Then I'll bring it back *here*."

And his fib fooled the child. Then he patted her head
And he got her a drink and he sent her to bed.
And when Cindy-Lou *Who* went to bed with her cup,
HE went to the chimney and stuffed the tree up!

Then the *last* thing he took
Was the log for their fire!
Then he went up the chimney, himself, the old liar.
On their walls he left nothing but hooks and some wire.

And the one speck of food
That he left in the house
Was a crumb that was even too small for a mouse.

Then

He did the *same* thing
To the *other Whos'* houses

Leaving crumbs
Much too small
For the other *Whos'* mouses!

It was quarter past dawn …
All the *Whos,* still a-bed,
All the *Whos*, still a-snooze
When he packed up his sled,
Packed it up with their presents! The ribbons! The wrappings!
The tags! And the tinsel! The trimmings! The trappings!

Three thousand feet up! Up the side of Mt. Crumpit,
He rode with his load to the tiptop to dump it!
"Pooh-Pooh to the *Whos*!" he was grinch-ish-ly humming.
"They're finding out now that no Christmas is coming!
"They're just waking up! I know just what they'll do!
"Their mouths will hang open a minute or two
"Then the *Whos* down in *Who*-ville will all cry BOO-HOO!"

"That's a noise," grinned the Grinch,
"That I simply MUST hear!"
So he paused. And the Grinch put his hand to his ear.
And he *did* hear a sound rising over the snow.
It started in low. Then it started to grow …

But the sound wasn't *sad*!
Why, this sound sounded *merry*!
It *couldn't* be so!
But it WAS merry! VERY!

He stared down at *Who*-ville!
The Grinch popped his eyes!
Then he shook!
What he saw was a shocking surprise!

Every *Who* down in *Who*-ville, the tall and the small,
Was singing! Without any presents at all!
He HADN'T stopped Christmas from coming!
IT CAME!
Somehow or other, it came just the same!

And the Grinch, with his grinch-feet ice-cold in the snow,
Stood puzzling and puzzling: "How *could* it be so?
"It came without ribbons! It came without tags!
"It came without packages, boxes or bags!"

And he puzzled three hours, till his puzzler was sore.
Then the Grinch thought of something he hadn't before!
"Maybe Christmas," he thought, "*doesn't* come from a store.
"Maybe Christmas … perhaps … means a little bit more!"

And what happened *then* …?
Well … in *Who*-ville they say
That the Grinch's small heart
Grew three sizes that day!
And the minute his heart didn't feel quite so tight,
He whizzed with his load through the bright morning light
And he brought back the toys! And the food for the feast!
And he …

… HE HIMSELF …!
The Grinch carved the roast beast!

ramshackle – klapprig ***a-snooze*** – *sleeping* **giddap** – *said to a horse to make it run* ***flue*** – Rauchfang ***to slither*** – *to move like a snake* ***slunk*** – *past of to slink* – schleichen ***pop gun*** – *toy gun that shoots a cork* ***nimbly*** – flink ***icebox*** – Kühlschrank ***glee*** – Freude ***to shove*** – *to push* ***fake*** – *not real* ***fib*** – *lie* ***ribbon*** – Band ***wrapping*** – Geschenkpapier ***tag*** – Anhänger ***tinsel*** – Lametta ***trimmings*** – *decorations* **trappings** – Drum und Dran

THE NIGHT BEFORE CHRISTMAS

by Clement C. Moore

THE NIGHT BEFORE CHRISTMAS

A drill, a hammer, an angry roar –
Our basement yields familiar noise:
It's Santa Daddy at grips once more
With those "easy to assemble" toys.

Rosemarie Williamson

Adapted as a song by Ruth Artman

A fat, jolly old man with a white beard filling stockings on Christmas Eve and reindeer flying through the sky pulling a sleigh full of toys – those familiar images of Christmas all became popular through one poem which an American professor of Hebrew and Greek, Clement C. Moore, wrote for his children in 1822.

The story goes that on Christmas Eve, Moore set out in a sleigh in the heavy snow to deliver Christmas presents. Peter, the family's Dutch handyman, was driving the sleigh. When Moore saw Peter's rosy cheeks and his twinkling eyes in the snowy moonlight, he was inspired to use that picture in his poem about Saint Nick.

There had been stories about flying reindeer in some old Nordic myths, but it was Moore who gave the eight reindeer their now-familiar names. (Their colleague Rudolph didn't join the team until 117 years later.)

Dutch immigrants had brought to America their stories of St. Nicholas, who brought gifts on the eve of December 6. In Moore's poem, he's called "Saint Nick" but his delivery date has been changed to December 24. The Dutch name "Sinterklaas" eventually became Americanized to Santa Claus. Today most children assume that "Santa" is his first name and "Claus" is his last name.

to nestle – kuscheln ***kerchief*** – Kopftuch ***clatter*** – Geklapper ***shutters*** – Fensterläden ***sash*** – Schiebefenster ***bound*** – Sprung ***jerk*** – Ruck ***nod*** – Nicken ***down of a thistle*** – Distelwolle ***ere*** – before

'Twas the night before Christmas, when all through the house,
Not a creature was stirring, not even a mouse;
The stockings were hung by the chimney with care,
In hopes that St Nicholas soon would be there.

The children were nestled all snug in their beds,
While visions of sugarplums danced in their heads;
And ma in her kerchief, and I in my cap,
Had just settled our brains for a long winter's nap.

When out on the lawn there arose such a clatter,
I sprang from my bed to see what was the matter.
Away to the window I flew like a flash!
Tore open the shutters and threw up the sash!

The moon was shining on the snow, the sky was all aglow;
When all at once I saw them appear:
A sleigh! And eight reindeer!

Who was that? Could it really be?
'Twas a little old driver, lively and quick;
I knew in a moment it was St Nick;
And oh, those reindeer, how they came,
And he called them all by name.
"Now Dasher! Now Dancer! Now Prancer and Vixen!
You're a little bit slow! On Comet! On Cupid!
On Donner and Blitzen! Come on, you guys, let's go!

And then I heard on the roof ...
The prancing of each little hoof;
As I was turning around,
Saint Nick came down the chimney with a bound!

He spoke not a word, but went straight to his work!
And filled all the stockings; then turned with a jerk!
And laying his finger aside of his nose,
And giving a nod, up the chimney he rose!

He sprang to his sleigh, to his team gave a whistle,
And away they all flew like the down of a thistle.
But I heard him exclaim, ere he drove out of sight,
"Merry Christmas to all and to all a goodnight".

WHY DO WE DECEIVE OUR CHILDREN EACH CHRISTMAS ABOUT SANTA CLAUS?

by Joel Achenbach

THERE ARE FIVE REASONS

ONE: Because as parents we enjoy the ruse as much as our children do. In a world of doubt and pain and well-founded cynicism we can for a moment, vicariously experience the rapture of believing that somewhere there is a being who cares for us so much and so selflessly that he will personally deliver sacks of gifts to our home on Christmas Eve, asking nothing in return but that we be good.

TWO: Because we fear our own mortality and thus do not want our children to grow up too rapidly. We want to keep them in an innocent state of Santa-belief. So obvious is our desire that often our kids will pretend to still believe in order that they not disappoint us.

THREE: Because as parents we have a hard enough time getting kids to behave properly and therefore employ Santa, an omniscient and personable God-like figure, as an extension of our authority.

FOUR: Because we intuitively understand what has been verified by *Hippocrates* magazine in a poll of two hundred child psychiatrists, and also supported by academic research at the University of Texas, the University of Chicago, and Cornell. It is good for young children to believe the world is filled with fantastic, benign, caring beings; that parents are not taking advantage of the child's gullibility as long as we do not lie outright when questioned directly; that the discovery of the Santa Claus deception is actually a positive revelation for about two in three children, who can feel pride in their acquired wisdom and can bond with their parents when upholding the myth for younger siblings.

'The trouble is that I don't believe in myself.'

FIVE: Because through ritual and tradition we try to transcend our temporal limits, straining to connect with past generations (in this case all the way back to the fourth century, when a bishop named Nicholas in the town of Myra in Asia Minor purportedly saved three impoverished girls from a life of prostitution by anonymously throwing purses of gold coins through the open window of their house) and to generations future. Though our own time is short, we can collectively breathe eternal life into our surrogate, Santa Claus, who will nobly represent our culture, carry on our good works, and offer comfort and the possibility of miracles to the little children who must inherit the earth.

deceive – betrügen ***ruse*** – *trick* ***vicariously*** – stellvertretend ***rapture*** – Entzücken ***mortality*** – Sterblichkeit ***omniscient*** – allwissend ***personable*** – *friendly* ***extension*** – Verlängerung ***poll*** – Umfrage ***benign*** – gütig ***to take advantage of something*** – etwas ausnutzen ***gullibility*** – Leichtgläubigkeit ***to bond*** – *to connect* ***sibling*** – Geschwister ***purportedly*** – angeblich ***impoverished*** – *very poor* ***inherit*** – erben

What if there really was a Santa Claus?

If there really was a Santa Claus

... animal activists would accuse him of making reindeer behave in unnatural ways such as flying rather than running.

... fitness experts would say that his weight problem set a bad example for children who already eat too many chips and chocolate bars.

... the fashion industry would insist that he should start wearing something more up-to-date instead of that old-fashioned red suit.

... homeowners would sue him for roof damage by reindeer hooves and a heavy sleigh.

... talk show hosts would bombard him with questions about his relationship to Mrs Claus and how she feels about having to spend Christmas Eve alone every year.

... labour union officials would inspect the working conditions of all those little elves making toys all year round in below-zero weather at the North Pole.

... income-tax collectors would question his source of income which enables him to produce such an unlimited supply of toys year after year.

Maybe it's better that good old Santa just exists as a spirit.

A SCIENTIFIC ANALYSIS OF SANTA CLAUS

1. No known species of reindeer can fly. But there are 300,000 species of living organisms yet to be classified, and while most of these are insects and germs, this does not completely rule out flying reindeer, which only Santa has ever seen.

2. There are two billion children (persons under 18) in the world. But since Santa doesn't handle the Muslim, Hindu, Jewish and Buddhist children, that reduces the caseload to 15 % of the total – 378 million according to the Population Reference Bureau. At an average of 3.5 children per household, that's 91.8 million homes. One presumes there's at least one good child in each home.

3. Santa has 31 hours of Christmas to work with, thanks to the different time zones and the rotation of the earth, assuming he travels east to west (which seems logical). This works out to 822.6 visits per second. This is to say that for each Christian household with good children, Santa has 1/1000th of a second to park, hop out of the sleigh, jump down the chimney, fill the stockings, distribute the presents under the tree, eat whatever snacks have been left, get back up the chimney, get back into the sleigh, and move on to the next house. Assuming that each of these 91.8 million stops are evenly distributed around the earth, (which of course we know to be false), we are now talking about 0.78 miles per household, a total trip of 75.5 million miles, not counting stops, to do what most of us must do at least once every 31 hours. This means that Santa's sleigh is moving at 650 miles per second, 3000 times the speed of sound. For purposes of comparison, the fastest man-made vehicle, the Ulysses space probe, moves at a poky 27.4 miles per second. A conventional reindeer can run 15 miles per hour.

4. The weight on the sleigh adds another interesting element. Assuming that each child gets nothing more than a medium-sized Lego set (2 pounds), the sleigh is carrying 321,300 tons, not counting Santa, who is invariably described as overweight. On land, conventional reindeer can pull no more than 300 pounds. Even granting that flying reindeer could pull ten times the normal amount, we cannot do the job with eight, or even nine. We need 214,200 reindeer. This increases the weight, not even counting the weight of the sleigh, to 352,430 tons. Again for comparison, this is four times the weight of a large ocean-liner.

5. 353,000 tons traveling at 650 miles per second creates enormous air resistance. This will heat up the reindeer in the same fashion as spacecraft re-entering the atmosphere. The lead pair of reindeer will absorb 14.3 QUINTILLION joules of energy per second. Each. In short, they will burst into flames almost instantaneously, exposing the reindeer behind them, and creating a deafening sonic boom in their wake. The entire reindeer team will be vaporized within 4.26 thousandths of a second. Santa, meanwhile, will be subjected to centrifugal forces 17,260.06 times greater than gravity. A 250-pound Santa would be pinned to the back of his sleigh by 4,315,015 pounds of force.

6. The only way Santa and the reindeer could possibly survive this would be through the help of Rudolph's nose. It is highly probable that this unique nose is made of heat resistant material and becomes red hot from deflecting the air resistance around the sleigh and other reindeer, creating a protective envelope similar to what is commonly known as "drafting" in automobile racing. This would also explain why they all live at the North Pole, as it takes one year of subzero temperatures to cool down Rudolph's nose before making the trip again.

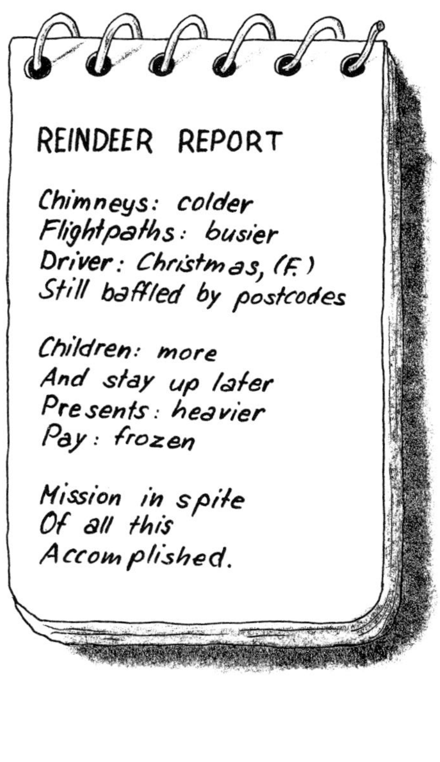

PERFECT PRESENT

If you're looking for something unusual to send
As a present this Christmas to some good old friend,
I think you will find that an excellent gift
Is a Fluff-footed, Frizzle-topped, Three-fingered Zifft.
A fine gift to give in all giving seasons,
He makes a fine present for twenty-three reasons.
The first reason is: He won't talk in his sleep.
The second one is that his food is quite cheap.
The third reason is: If you go anywhere
You can take him along on the train for half fare.
The fourth reason is: He is friendly with eagles
And won't pick a fight with your neighbourhood beagles.
The fifth reason is: When you talk on the phone
He won't make a racket or blow a trombone.
The sixth reason is that this wonderful pet
Doesn't smell terribly bad when he's wet
And the rest of the reasons I sort of forget,
But I certainly do recommend as a gift
The Fluff-footed, Frizzle-topped,
Three-fingered Zifft.

Dr. Seuss

Message to Santa

P U Z Z L E

What is the little girl saying to Santa?

Solve the puzzle to find out.

L	I	A	T	Y	N	O	P	C	A
B	D	U	C	A	C	Z	O	B	Y
W	N	O	S	E	A	M	X	E	W
O	M	Y	V	B	P	T	F	A	X
R	C	M	U	L	S	P	Q	R	K
R	D	O	E	C	H	I	L	D	N
O	E	T	L	I	S	T	R	M	E
M	E	H	H	'	I	A	O	N	E
O	F	E	G	L	B	O	O	T	S
T	J	R	?	L	!	C	D	O	R

1. Go to the fifth column. Count seven boxes from the top. Read the word that begins there and ends at the bottom of the puzzle.
2. Find the fourth row. Read the last three letters in this row.
3. It's a three-letter word that ends in the second row, third column.
4. It's a two-letter word that begins in the fourth box of the second column.
5. Begin at the next to last box of the top row. Read diagonally from right to left.
6. The word begins in a box that is in the fourth column, fourth box from the bottom.
7. Begin in the lower left corner and read from bottom to top.

______ ______ ______ ______ ______ ______ ______.
1 2 3 4 5 6 7

There are ten other words hidden in the puzzle. All are things you can see in the picture.

LONG WALK PART OF GIFT

The African boy listened carefully as the teacher explained why it is that Christians give presents to each other on Christmas Day. "The gift is an expression of our joy over the birth of Jesus and our friendship for each other," she said. When Christmas Day came, the boy brought the teacher a sea shell of lustrous beauty. "Where did you ever find such a beautiful shell?" the teacher asked as she gently fingered the gift. The youth told her that there was only one spot where such extraordinary shells could be found. When he named the place, a certain bay several miles away, the teacher was left speechless. "Why ... why, it's gorgeous ... wonderful, but you shouldn't have gone all that way to get a gift for me." His eyes brightening, the boy answered, "Long walk part of gift."

Gerald Horton Bath

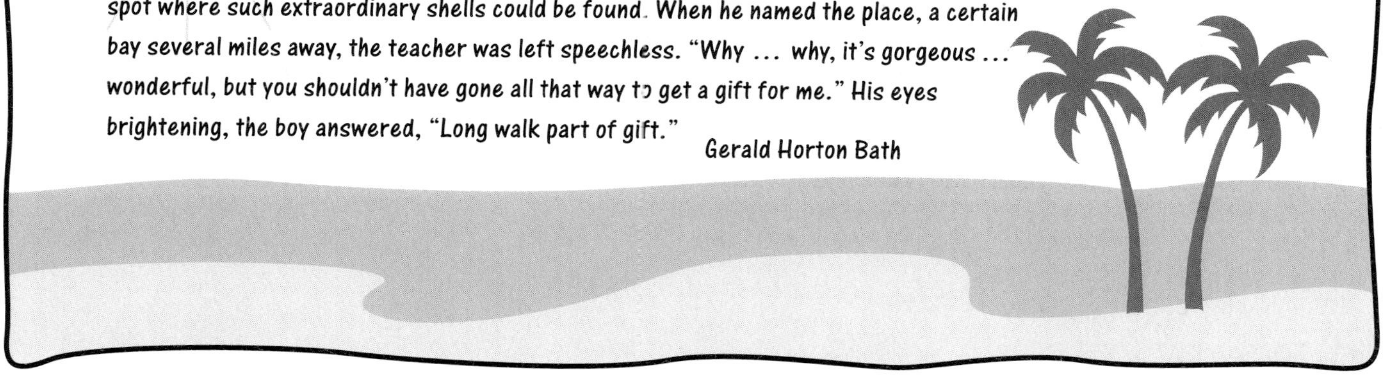

Giving

To solve this puzzle, answer the clues below. Put the letters from those words into the main puzzle grid at the corresponding number. The message is a quote about giving, written by the Lebanese-American philosopher Khalil Gibran (1883-1931).

1. Traditional English Christmas plant

___ ___ ___ ___ ___
50 54 11 68 74

2. Question word

___ ___ ___
17 71 81

3. Plant that doesn't lose its leaves in winter

___ ___ ___ ___ -
7 84 19 65

___ ___ ___ ___ ___
4 33 51 38 20

4. Favourite child's gift

___ ___ ___
46 63 30

5. Twelve inches

___ ___ ___ ___
61 2 28 77

6. Use a gun

___ ___ ___ ___ ___
36 18 22 42 70

7. Not normal

___ ___ ___ ___ ___ ___ ___
3,23 43 79 66 64 72 80

8. Henry XIII had six of them

___ ___ ___ ___ ___
49 5,47 58 67 48

9. Small piece

___ ___ ___
8 12 73

10. Opposite of receiving

___ ___ ___ ___ ___ ___
24 83 6 57 52 56

11. Design

___ ___ ___ ___ ___
37 14 1 15 59

12. Not hard

___ ___ ___ ___
40 31 69 13

13. Positive answer

___ ___ ___
53 16 44

14. Not the bottom

___ ___ ___
10 35 34

15. Exists

___ ___
25 39

16. Pronoun, second person

___ ___ ___
21 60 9,55

17. Flying saucer

___ ___ ___
76,32 29 75

18. American soldier

___ ___
82 41

19. Each

___ ___ ___ ___ ___
27 26 85 78 62

20. Me

___
45

1	2	3	■	4	5	6	7	■	8	9	10	■	11	12	13	14	15	16
17	18	19	20	■	21	22	23	■	24	25	26	27	■	28	29	■	■	■
30	31	32	33	■	34	35	36	37	38	39	40	41	42	43	44	●	■	■
45	46	■	47	48	■	49	50	51	52	■	53	54	55	■	56	57	58	59
60	61	■	62	63	64	65	66	67	68	69	■	70	71	72	73	■	■	■
74	75	76	■	77	78	79	80	81	■	82	83	84	85	●	■	■	■	■

DEAR SANTA CLAUS

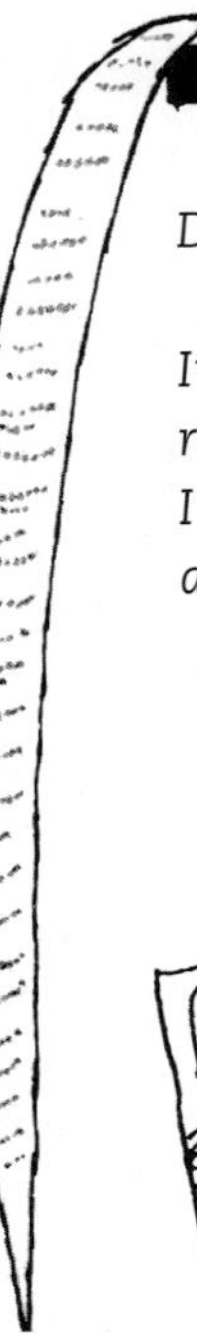

Jack Prelutsky

Dear Santa Claus,

It's me again
reminding you I'm here,
I'm making my list easier
and shorter than last year.

I'd like a stack of comic books,
a dozen apple pies,
a box of chocolate brownies,
and an elephant that flies,
a porpoise for the bathtub
and a dragon for my room,
a robot that does homework
and can also use a broom.

And I'd like a hippopotamus,
a trumpet, and a drum,
I could use a half a dollar
and a million sticks of gum.

Just leave them underneath our tree
or near our fireplace,
Oh! you probably won't bring them,
but I'm writing ... just in case.

Unscramble the letters to find out what's in the Christmas packages.

CHRISTMAS THANK-YOUS

Mick Gowar

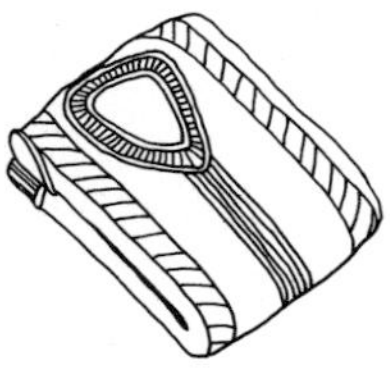

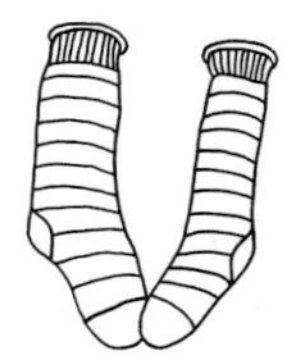

Dear Auntie,
Oh, what a nice jumper
I've always adored powder blue
and fancy you thinking of
orange and pink
for the stripes
how clever of you!

Dear Uncle,
The soap is
terrific
So
useful
and such a kind thought and
how did you guess that
I'd just used the last of
the soap that last Christmas brought?

Dear Gran,
Many thanks for the hankies
Now I really can't wait for the flu
and the daisies embroidered
in red round the 'M'
for Michael
how
thoughtful of you!

Dear Cousin,
What socks!
and the same sort you wear
so you must be
the last word in style
and I'm certain you're right that the
luminous green
WILL make me stand out a mile.

Dear Sister,
I quite understand your concern
it's a risk sending jam in the post
But I think I've pulled out
all the big bits
of glass
so it won't taste too sharp
spread on toast.

Dear Grandad,
Don't fret
I'm delighted
So DON'T think your gift will
offend
I'm not at all hurt
that you gave up this year
and just sent me
a fiver
to spend.

THE TWELVE DAYS OF CHRISTMAS

English traditional

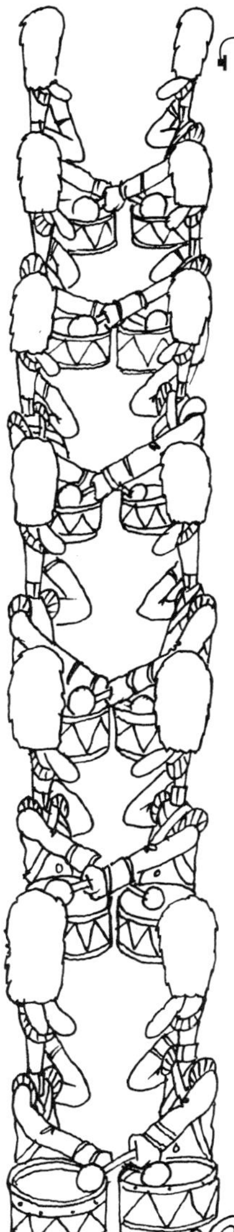

On the first day of Christmas, my true love sent to me,
A partridge in a pear tree.

On the second day of Christmas, my true love sent to me,
Two turtle doves, and a partridge in a pear tree.

On the third day of Christmas, my true love sent to me,
Three French hens, two turtle doves,
and a partridge in a pear tree.

fourth day … four calling birds
fifth day … five gold rings
sixth day … six geese a-laying
seventh day … seven swans a-swimming
eighth day … eight maids a-milking
ninth day … nine ladies dancing
tenth day … ten lords a-leaping
eleventh day … eleven pipers piping
twelfth day … twelve drummers drumming

THE TWELVE DAYS OF

by Sandra Harris

The Studio,
16 1/2 Belgrave Mews West,
London SW1

26 DECEMBER

My tender true love,

Your gift arrived only this morning and I am overwhelmed. How chic! How charming! How original! A PARTRIDGE *– and in its own little pear tree. You are too divine.*
Your own love,

PS Would Fortnums stock partridge food?

27 DECEMBER

Angel of my heart,

How little I really know you, even after three whole weeks. Imagine, I thought my dear partridge and its sweet pear tree was it. My Christmas present. Silly me. This morning I am greeted by not one turtle dove, but two. Is this symbolic? I wait to hear the answer from your own dear lips.

Your adoring one,

28 DECEMBER

Dearest,

What can I say? There I was, feeding my partridge (Fortnums were as reliable as ever) and admiring my turtle doves, which are lovely if just a little over-enthusiastic with all that cooing, when I am amazed, yet again, by a further gift. Three French hens. Fancy. Or as Mother put it, "Tiens!" Of course, we adore them but can't help wondering exactly where to put them. The studio has always seemed quite spacious, but with our new feathered friends it is suddenly less so. These extravagant gestures are charming but don't you think it is really THE THOUGHT *that counts?*

Your loving friend,

P.S. I have ordered a sack of mixed bird food from Fortnums to cover general requirements. Will this be adequate in your view?

29 DECEMBER

Darling,

Tsk, tsk. Divine, generous, lavish as you are I must draw a halt. You probably didn't notice (funny old thing) that actually the studio is MINUSCULE. *Mother and I have often discussed this and how we really have no room to swing a cat, let alone ten birds. You did realise there are ten now, did you? I mean, the four calling birds only arrived today. It has been quite a challenge to manage them all in a flat with a "no pets" clause. I could use Mother to explain the clucking and the cooing, but the squawking is just a shade too piercing, even for Mother. She has retired to her room with one of her heads. I would love to do the same but the French hens got there first. Next time I'd like them* AFTER *they have become duvets.*

Cordially yours,

30 DECEMBER

My dear,

Listen, I absolutely love the rings. I can't believe how you thought of them after all these birds, but I am thrilled to get such a normal present. Forgive me, but while the partridge and the turtle doves and the French hens and the calling birds are terribly interesting they are becoming just a little wearing. Perhaps you noticed from the tone of my last letter. Mother is back on form and disapproves. She says a gold ring at this stage in our relationship is far too previous. I agree. ONE *gold ring would be. Five, on the other hand, or indeed any hand, are just too divine. And now, my dear love, please do not think you have to continue to astound me with your gifts. I am wholly and completely satisfied.*

Your loving one,

31 DECEMBER

Dear Sir,

Have you gone quite mad? Over the last five days - five of the most chaotic days of my life, I might add – I have become used to the cooing and clucking and squawking all day and all night. When you live in the only aviary in Mayfair you have little choice, so I didn't notice the HISSING. *Not at first. But there they were. Six geese sitting on my doorstep. And they're a'laying. Do you have any idea how inconvenient it is to have six geese a'laying at this time of year? I am at my wits' end to think of why you thought I could want six geese. Or, for that matter, four calling birds, three French hens and two turtle doves. I am still quite fond of the partridge but the five gold rings would have been perfectly acceptable on their own. I beg you.* NO MORE GIFTS.

Courteously yours,

CHRISTMAS

1 JANUARY

Sir,

What a way to spend New Year! I want these swans out of my bath by six o'clock. All seven of them. And while you're at it you can clear the French hens out of my bed, the turtle doves out of the airing cupboard and keep the calling birds away from Mother. They have caught in her hair net three times now. She has learned how to squawk. Particularly when she saw the neighbours' petition. It includes several INFLUENTIAL *signatures. For pity's sake, this is my* HOME*. Leave me alone!*

Yours in haste,

2 JANUARY

Listen, you wart-eared toad! I have had just about enough.

Two men in white coats have just been to take Mother away. My landlady has called a public meeting over the danger of slipping on goose eggs in the landing. My bathroom is like the first act of Swan Lake and I am now faced by eight maids! Do you know how rare this species is in Mayfair? That they are a'milking is immaterial. I have managed to distract them momentarily with back copies of Farmers Weekly *in the cupboard under the stairs but it can't last.*

3 JANUARY

Well, you've done it. The media are here. It seems I am harbouring a new breed of boat people. From the Isle of Wight perhaps? They got the wind up when the eight maids started Morris dancing in the front courtyard, but it was the nine pipers piping that really got the cables and the cameras into position. I am feeling strangely calm. I will confront whatever else you have in store for me with stoicism. England expects …

4 JANUARY

Mr Terry Wogan from the BBC has just been on the phone wanting to know if he can beam his television programme "live" from my little studio in Belgravia. It seems that the nation wants to know what is going on. So do I. I have just had to separate the nine pipers from the ten drummers which you so kindly sent this morning. I explained that your wish was obviously that they should pipe and drum and not fight over the milkmaids but I fear my words have gone unheeded. Please include a roll of barbed wire with your next gift and two dozen valium.

5 JANUARY

Did you see us on Wogan? All of us, I mean? The BBC were thrilled, they said. They usually have to supply the extras, they said, like pipers piping, drummers drumming, maids, that sort of things, not to mention our feathered friends, but I had everything laid on. How thoughtful, they said.

And they loved the eleven Lords a'leaping you forwarded this morning. So did the milkmaids. Barbed wire isn't what it's cracked up to be, is it?

6 JANUARY

I have been asked by Mr Norris McWhirter of The Guinness Book of Records *if I would like to be included. It seems that 23 birds and 39 adults in one mews flat is a new world record. I was about to give the go-ahead when the twelve ladies dancing arrived. They couldn't be left out. Not after missing all the excitement of the television, but I explained that you must know what you are doing. After all, no one else does. I have been advised to take a little break, so should you want to contact me I shall be at*

The Nunnery
Much Hounding In The Marsh
Little Codswallop
Hants.

PS Next year just send scent. Poison by Christian Dior will be ideal. On second thought, don't send it, drink it.

studio** – small flat **mews** – row of flats **divine** – wonderful **Fortnums** – high-class store noted for exotic foods **to coo** – to make a soft noise **tiens** – French exclamation, oh dear **spacious** – having enough room **minuscule** – very small* ***let alone – geschweige denn ***a shade** – a little bit **piercing** – sharp and loud **head** – (sl) headache **duvet** – feather-filled bed cover **wearing** – tiring **previous** – (sl)* voreilig ***aviary** – place where birds are kept **at wits' end** – not knowing what to do **petition** – formal written request **for pity's sake** – idiom used to express anger or surprise **wart-eared toad*** – warzenohrige Kröte ***landing** – area at the top of stairs **immaterial** – not important **back copies** – old magazines **to harbour** – to give a home to **breed** – kind **boat people** – refugees **Isle of Wight** – island off the south coast of England **to get the wind up** – to become frightened **Morris dance** – traditional dance with bells and sticks **stoicism** – ability to endure pain **Belgravia** – fashionable district of London **unheeded*** – unbeachtet ***barbed wire*** – Stacheldraht ***nunnery*** – Nonnenkloster

THE  GIFT OF THE MAGI

Based on a short story by O. Henry

DELLA: One dollar and eighty-seven cents. Let me count it once more. One dollar and eighty-seven cents. And tomorrow is Christmas Day. What can I buy my Jim with only one dollar and eighty-seven cents? I do want a special present for him, something fine and rare. But what can I buy with only one dollar and eighty-seven cents?

NARRATOR: Della stood up and looked sadly out the window at a grey cat walking a grey fence in a grey backyard. Jim wouldn't be home from work for several hours. But what could she get him if she only had a dollar and eighty-seven cents? Twenty dollars a week didn't go very far, especially now that they had to pay eight dollars a week for their simple little flat. Suddenly Della caught sight of her own reflection in the window and she knew what she could do. Quickly she pulled down her hair and let it fall to its full length.

Now, I must tell you that there were two possessions in which Jim and Della Young both took a mighty pride. One was Jim's gold watch that had been his father's and grandfather's. The other was Della's hair. It was long and beautiful and fell about her now like a cascade of brown waters. She looked once more at her reflection, not noticing a tear or two that dropped on the worn red carpet. Then she quickly did her hair up again and reached for her old brown jacket and her old brown hat. With a sparkle in her eyes she ran down the steps and didn't stop until she came to a shop where a sign read: 'Mme Sofronie. Hair Goods of All Kinds.'

DELLA: Will you buy my hair?

MADAME: I buy hair. Take your hat off and let's have a look at it. Mmmmm. Twenty dollars.

DELLA: Give it to me quick.

NARRATOR: The next two hours flew by on rosy wings as Della went from one shop to the next looking for the perfect present. At last she found it. It surely had been made for Jim and no one else. It was a platinum chain, simple in design. It was like him. Quietness and value – the description applied to both. Twenty-one dollars they took from her for it, and she hurried home with the eighty-seven cents. Della still had an hour before Jim would be home. She took out her curling irons and lighted the gas and went to work repairing the ravages made by generosity added to love. Which is always a tremendous task. Within forty minutes her head was covered with tiny close-lying curls that made her look wonderfully like a schoolboy. She looked at her reflection in the mirror long, carefully, and critically.

DELLA: If Jim doesn't kill me before he takes a second look at me, he'll say I look like a Coney Island chorus girl. But what could I do – oh! what could I do with a dollar and eighty-seven cents?

NARRATOR: At seven o'clock the coffee was made and the frying pan was on the back of the stove hot and ready to cook the chops. Jim was never late.

DELLA: Please God, make him think I am still pretty.

JIM *coming in the door:* Della …

DELLA: Jim, darling, don't look at me that way. I had my hair cut off and sold it because I couldn't have lived through Christmas without giving you a present. It'll grow out again. I just had to do it. My hair grows awfully fast. Say 'Merry Christmas' Jim, and let's be happy. You don't know what a beautiful gift I've got for you.

JIM: You've cut off your hair?

DELLA: Cut if off and sold it. Don't you like me just as well, anyhow? I'm me without my hair, ain't I?

JIM: You say your hair is gone?

DELLA: You needn't look for it. It's sold. I tell you – sold and gone, too. It's Christmas Eve, boy. Be good to me, for it went for you. Maybe the hairs of my head were numbered, but nobody could ever count my love for you. Shall I put the chops on, Jim?

JIM: Don't make a mistake, Dell, about me. I don't think there's anything in the way of a haircut or a shampoo that could make me like my girl any less. But if you'll unwrap that package you may see why you had me going a while at first.

DELLA: Oh Jim, the combs. – The ones I've looked at so often in that Broadway window. Oh they're the most beautiful combs I've ever seen – and just the perfect colour to wear in my hair. *Sobs, then brighter.* My hair grows so fast, Jim! Oh, but now you have to see what I have for you. Isn't it a dandy, Jim? I hunted all over town to find it. You'll have to look at the time a hundred times a day now. Give me your watch. I want to see how it looks on it.

JIM: Dell, let's put our Christmas presents away and keep 'em for a while. They're too nice to use just at present. I sold the watch to get the money to buy your combs. And now suppose you put the chops on.

NARRATOR: The magi, as you know, were wise men – wonderfully wise men who brought gifts to the Babe in the manger. They invented the art of giving Christmas presents. Being wise, their gifts were no doubt wise ones. But here I have told you the story of two foolish children who most unwisely sacrificed for each other the greatest treasures of their house. But in a last word to the wise of these days, let it be said that of all who give and receive gifts, such as these two are the wisest. They are the magi.

Magi [ˈmeɪdʒaɪ] – Heilige Drei Könige ***curling iron*** – Lockenschere ***ravages*** – Verwüstung ***Coney Island*** – *amusement park in New York* ***to have somebody going*** – *to confuse somebody* ***a dandy*** – *something wonderful* ***to sacrifice*** – opfern

SNOWMAN, SNOWFLAKES AND SNOWBALLS

Find one word which goes together with all the words in each group. For example: _____man, _____flake, _____storm, _____ball, _____shoes
The answer is SNOW.

"We have to go back. This is my laundry bag."

1. Christmas_____, _____ game, post _____, _____board, birthday_____
2. film_____, _____fish, shooting_____, _____board, _____trek
3. _____feet, _____turkey, _____blood, _____war, _____front
4. _____Cross _____head, _____tape, _____carpet, _____wood
5. _____weight, high_____, _____bulb, _____house, _____year
6. cow_____, _____flower, door_____, _____bottoms, _____boy
7. _____horn, _____back, _____peace, _____house, _____belt
8. Christmas _____, _____top, _____frog, _____house, family_____
9. dry _____, _____Age,

cube, _____skate, _____cream

For each category on the left, think of a word that begins with the letter at the top of the column. The first one is done for you. You get one point for each word you can think of, and one extra point for each word you have that no one else in your group chose.

✱	S	T	A	R
Word that has something to do with Christmas	Santa Claus			
Something that could be a Christmas gift				
Something to eat				
Country				
Singer or pop group				
Word that ends with the letter "e"				
Girl's name				

A plant with shiny green leaves and bright red berries. In England, people have decorated their houses with it for hundreds of years.	The tradition started in Germany. In Britain and the US they are decorated with coloured balls and lights but rarely with real candles.	Many people send 50 – 100 of these to all their friends and relatives. They are displayed in the house, hanging on a string or taped to a door.	A plant that doesn't touch the earth, but grows in other trees. People thought it was magic. Today you can can kiss anyone who stands under it.	A place to put food for animals. The baby Jesus slept in one 2000 years ago. There's a well-known English Christmas carol about it.	They are made of paper and contain little gifts, jokes and paper hats. In Britain, people pull them open and wear the hats during their Christmas dinner.
They go from house to house singing Christmas songs. They usually collect money or get something special to eat or drink.	He has a white beard, dresses in red and brings gifts for Christmas. He lives at the North Pole and spends the year making toys.	This animal usually lives in the northern woods. On Christmas Eve it can fly and pull a sleigh loaded with Christmas presents.	It is round and made of holly leaves or other evergreens. It hangs on the front door and often has a big red bow.	Part of every traditional Christmas dinner in Britain. It's dark, round, heavy, full of dried fruit and eaten hot with brandy butter.	Before people had cars they travelled over ice and snow in one of these. Santa packs the presents in one on Christmas Eve.
They can keep your feet warm, but on Christmas Eve children also have a special one they hang up for Santa, who fills it with gifts during the night.	It's a big bird, originally from America, which lots of people like to eat for Christmas dinner.	Most people open these on Christmas morning. They are usually wrapped in colourful paper and contain nice surprises.	It's on the roof of a house and smoke comes out of it. Santa climbs down it when he brings the presents.	It's a thick piece of wood traditionally burnt in the fireplace at Christmas. There are also Christmas cakes made in this shape.	Lots of English Christmas cards have pictures of this little bird with a red breast.

SANTA CLAUS FATHER CHRISTMAS	REINDEER	STOCKING	PRESENTS	CHRISTMAS PUDDING	HOLLY
CRACKERS	MISTLETOE	YULE LOG	WREATH	MANGER	SLEIGH
CHRISTMAS CARDS	TURKEY	CAROL SINGERS	ROBIN	CHRISTMAS TREE	CHIMNEY

CHRISTMAS COUNTDOWN

☆ **You will need:**
the pictures on this page,
2 large pieces of paper or thin cardboard,
glue, scissors,
coloured pencils
or felt pens.

☆ Colour the 24 pictures and cut them out.
☆ Glue all the pictures to a large piece of paper leaving some space between the pictures.
☆ Decorate your paper with your own drawings or designs.
☆ Use the 24 pictures as doors. Cut them on 3 sides.
Put a number from 1 to 24 on each door in mixed up order.
☆ Take the second piece of paper or cardboard and put a little bit of glue around all four edges. Stick the 2 pieces of paper together.
☆ Think up little surprises to put behind each door: a joke, message, little poem, promise, a scrambled word, picture . . .
☆ Give your Advent calendar to a special friend!

How to make an Advent Calendar

STRANGE

A RATHER STRANGE LIVING-ROOM

Describe the picture and see how many unusual things you can find.

FIND SOMEONE WHO ...

★ can say "Merry Christmas" in three languages ____________________

★ is going to eat turkey this year at Christmas ____________________

★ has ever spent Christmas in a foreign country ____________________

★ has ever been given an animal as a Christmas present ____________________

★ is wearing something red today ____________________

★ can play ice hockey ____________________

★ has made a snowman this year ____________________

★ has a birthday near Christmas ____________________

★ knows how to ride a snowboard ____________________

★ has ridden in a one-horse open sleigh ____________________

Mystery Picture

Colour the boxes to find the mystery picture.

1	cake	bread	sugar	carrote	milk	turkey	cheese	beans	butter
2	hat	jeans	shirt	shoe	boot	sock	coat	dress	jacket
3	sun	moon	stars	pen	pig	pencil	cloud	rain	snow
4	finger	elbow	eyes	cow	mouth	chin	lips	arm	leg
5	Philip	Alex	May	April	August	Sunday	July	George	Peter
6	potato	apple	orange	meat	peach	banana	kiwi	cherry	peas
7	China	Paris	Oslo	London	Tokyo	Cairo	Thames	Chicago	Turkey
8	red	cold	green	blue	hot	pink	white	warm	black
9	Charles	William	Albert	Sarah	Liz	Vicky	Anne	George	Diana
10	one	two	three	four	count	five	six	seven	eight
11	in	at	on	tc	over	an	go	be	is
12	boy	girl	bird	table	dog	chair	man	farmer	nurse

1. Find row 7. Colour the cities green and the rivers red.
2. Go to row 5. Make all days of the week red. Co our the months green.
3. In row 12 colour everything blue that has four egs.
4. In row 1 colour all things to drink yellow.
5. Find the names in row 9. Colour them green.
6. Find row 2. Colour everything green that you can put on your feet.
7. Go to row 11. Colour all words black that have more than two letters.
8. In row 3 colour all things green that you can write with. Colour all animals red.
9. Now go to row 4. Colour everything green that is part of a face. Make all animals red.
10. In row 6 colour all fruit green. Make everything red that is not a fruit or a vegetable.
11. Go to row 8. Make all the colours green and all other words red.
12. And now go to row 10. Make all the words that aren't numbers black.

CHRISTMAS CROSSWORD PUZZLE

ACROSS

2 Can be made of snow or gingerbread
4 Christmas song
6 Doctor of Medicine, short form
7 Morning
8 People sometimes get Christmas gifts that they can't ______
10 Member of Parliament
11 When you open a nice present you can say 'oh' and ______
13 Is, am, are
14 Continent
16 Joseph's wife
17 Something to watch
18 English children leave it early on Dec. 25
20 Part of a face
22 Rudolph's nose
24 At the beginning of a word such as president or wife, it means former or not any more
25 Little word used with home, noon, and last
27 Boss of a large firm, short for Chief Executive Officer
29 There was a very bright one over Bethlehem
31 Door decoration at Christmas
32 Did you _____ your bed today?
33 Before a man's name
34 Short for the British Standards Institution
35 Place for experiments
37 Not she
38 Time for Guy Fawkes' Day in England and Thanksgiving Day in the USA (short form)
40 Everyone has two
42 Weather at the North Pole
43 Not far
45 Not on
46 Before Christ
47 See you (funny short form)
49 Reindeer pull it
52 Can sound like 'f' or nothing
54 Driver of a plane
56 You can find one in a classroom
58 Christmas plant
59 Needed for soup
60 Found in forests, and at Christmas in living-rooms (singular)

DOWN

1 British and American people se… lots of them in December
2 Mother
3 Negative answer
4 You can listen to it
5 City in California
8 When Santa is finished in a h…
9 Three to four months after C…
10 Happy, used often a…
12 Hello
13 University degree, short for Bachelor of Arts
15 Same as 25 across
19 Last month in the year
20 Tests
21 Each (short form)
23 Usually the first word in a letter
24 Film from the 1980s about a creature from another planet
26 The _____ Days of Christmas
28 Old Testament
30 Water from the sky
34 You often hear it at Christmas
36 Santa Claus _______ a lot of presents last year
37 When Santa laughs he says ______
39 One time
41 Used to be on cars from Finland
44 In pictures they often look like people with wings (singular)
46 American sandwich made with bacon, lettuce and tomatoes (short form)
48 Used for heating, also for making salads
49 Japanese bean and sauce
50 They say 'Buon Natale' there at Christmas
51 It keeps your head warm
53 Not his
54 Busy place before Christmas (short form)
55 Beginning of Lloyd and llama
57 When at the beginning of a word it often means 'again'

www.the-north-pole.com/santamail.html

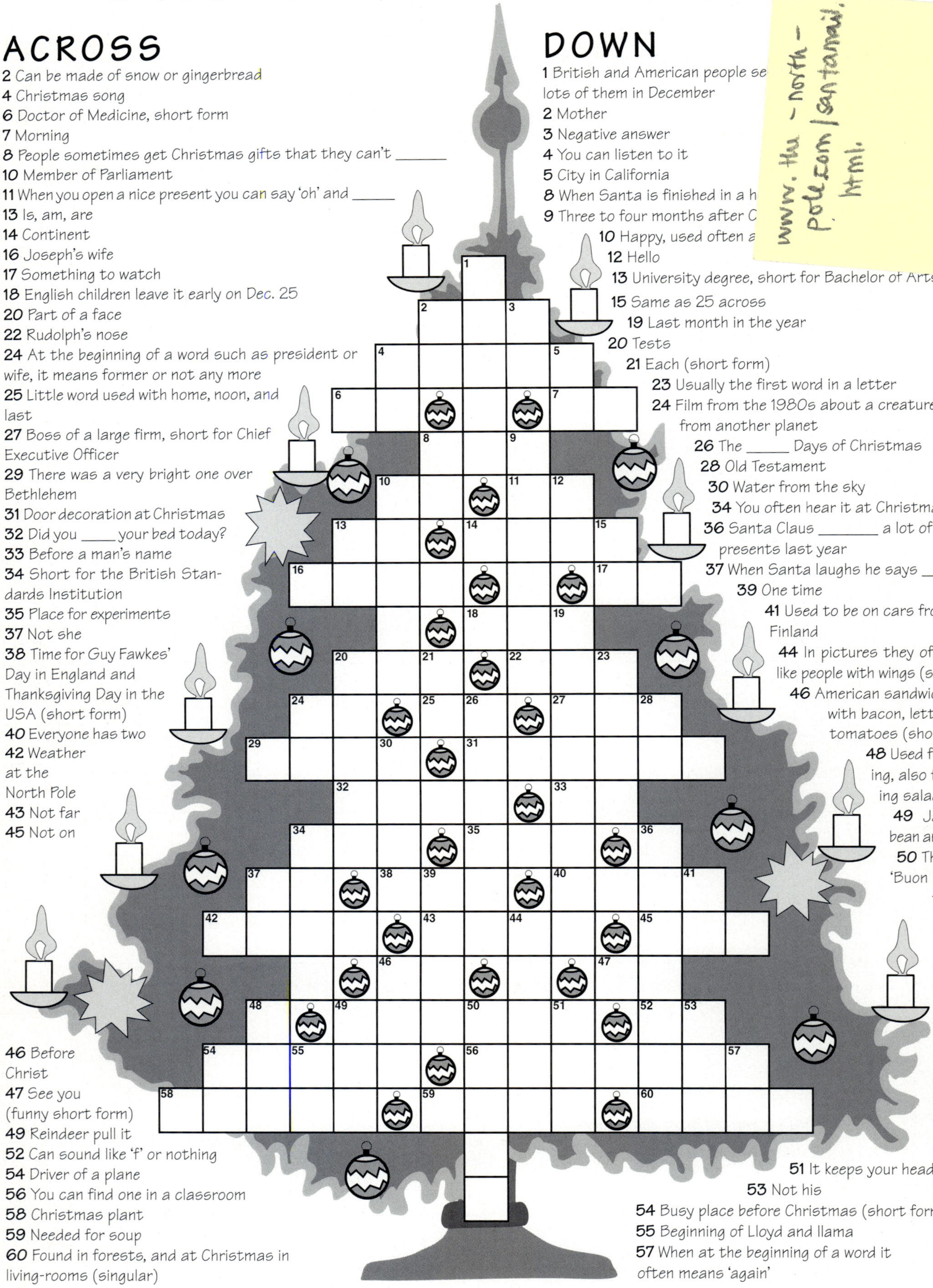

For 2–4 players. Take turns throwing the dice and move your markers. It is okay if two or more players are on the same square. To win, you must throw the exact number needed to land on **MERRY CHRISTMAS.**

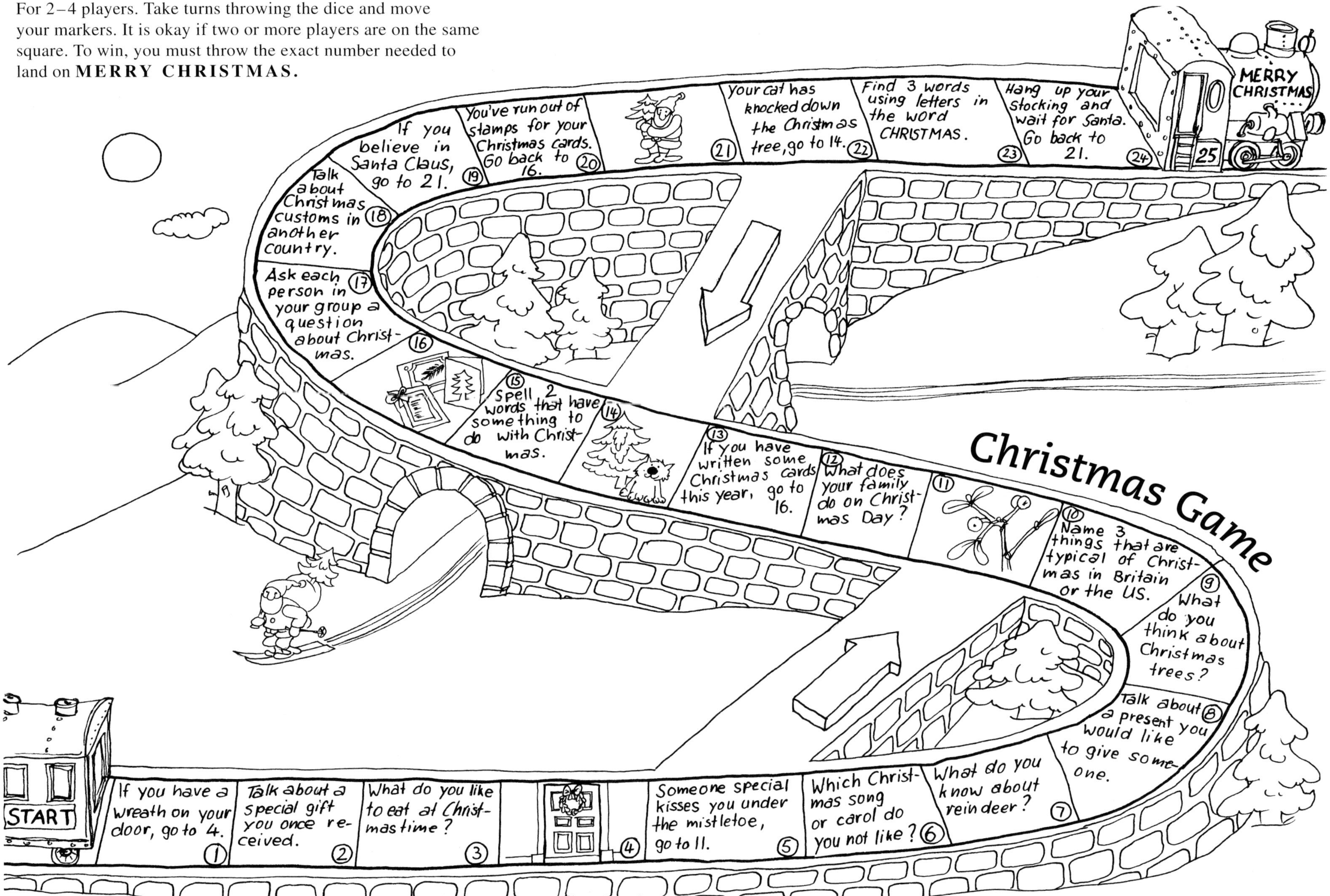

Would you like to have a

Christmas Party in your school?

WHEN could it be?

WHERE?

WHAT do you want to DO, EAT ...?

POPCORN CHAINS

In America the most traditional way to decorate a Christmas tree is with popcorn chains.
You will need: white thread, a sharp thin sewing needle, popcorn.
For best results use popcorn that is a day old (it doesn't break so easily).
It is also traditional to make chains with fresh cranberries together with the popcorn.

CANDY MOUSE

You will need: felt, needle and thread, cotton wool, string or yarn for the tail, wrapped sweets, 2 buttons.
Cut two pieces of felt in the shape of a mouse. Sew them together leaving a little hole. Stuff with cotton wool and sew together. Add a long tail. Tie some sweets – or a candy cane – to the tail.
Cut two circles for the ears and sew them on. Add the eyes.

Going Crackers

GOING CRACKERS

Gold earrings, whisky marmalade and leather credit-card holders are some of the gifts inside crackers which are sold by exclusive English shops at Christmastime. More traditional crackers contain cheap plastic toys, jokes and paper hats. But whatever is inside, crackers have been a favourite part of British Christmas celebrations since the 1840s, when a London baker began selling sweets wrapped in coloured paper with a message inside. They didn't sell too well until he added a "bang" to them, a chemically-treated strip that makes a popping sound when the cracker is pulled apart.
When two people pull a cracker, the one who holds the larger part when it breaks gets the things inside. In most crackers there is a paper hat, which British people then wear at the Christmas dinner table.

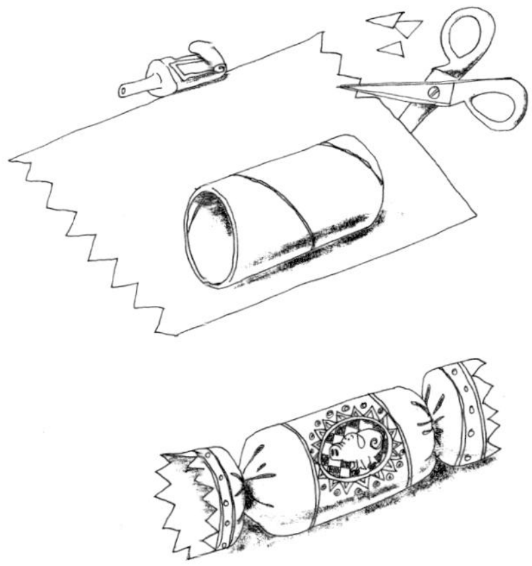

crackers – (BE infml) crazy

*
HOW TO MAKE A CRACKER
*

You will need:
crepe paper (30 cm x 20 cm), thread or gift ribbon, a cardboard tube (toilet paper roll), glue, bits of shiny paper, something to put inside: sweets, small gift, joke …

*

Lie the tube on the crepe paper with the crinkly lines going along the tube, not across it.

*

Roll the crepe paper around the tube. Use a little glue to hold it in place.

*

Put the presents inside. Tie the ends with thread or ribbon.

*

Decorate the cracker as you like by gluing on designs or strips of shiny paper.

CRACKER JOKES

What did Adam say on December 24?
What do robbers eat for Christmas dinner?
What is full of raisins and on a secret mission?
What's red, round, and goes up and down, up and down?
What do you give an octopus for Christmas?
Mother, can I have a canary for Christmas?

Beef-burglars.
No, we're having turkey this year.
Four pairs of gloves.
It's Christmas, Eve.
A cranberry on a lift.
Mince spy.

What goes "gobble, gobble, ha-ha-ha, BOOM"?
What did Santa say to the little chimney?
What do you call a blind reindeer?
We had my grandma and grandpa from Arizona for Christmas dinner.
What nationality is Santa?
Where did Mr and Mrs Snowman meet?

At the Snow Ball.
No eye deer.
Really? We had turkey.
You're too young to smoke.
North Polish.
A turkey exploding with laughter.

Have you ever seen a man-eating shark?
Can't you share your new sled with your brother?
What's red, round, and attracted to metal objects?
What did Santa say to his wife when he looked out the window?
What goes "gobble, gobble" and flies at 2000 miles per hour?
What do you call a man who claps at Christmas?

Look at the rain, dear.
A turkey on the Concorde.
No, but I've seen a man eating turkey – my dad last Christmas.
A magnetic cranberry.
Santapplause.
Of course. I take it downhill and he takes it uphill.

What do monkeys sing at Christmas?
Why is Christmas like a cat on the beach?
What happened to the man who stole a calendar?
Doctor, I get a pain in my nose when I drink my tea.
What do you get if you cross Father Christmas with a detective?
Why is a couch like a turkey?

He got twelve months.
Jungle bells, jungle bells.
Santa Clues.
They are both stuffed.
They both have sandy claws.
Have you tried taking the spoon out?

Christmas

METAL FOIL ORNAMENTS

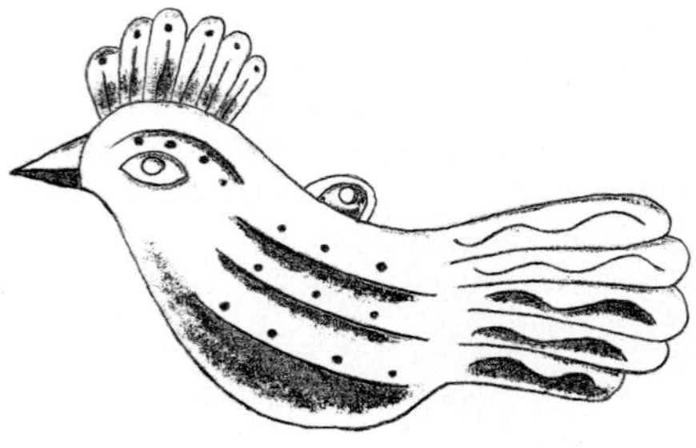

You will need: metal foil (from a craft shop), strong scissors, magazines (to make working surface softer), pencil, ballpoint pen with ink removed, string for hanging.
Make a pattern out of thick paper (bird, heart, bell, etc.). Place the pattern on the metal foil and draw around it with a soft pencil.
Place the foil on some magazines with the pattern on top as before. Go over the outline with the pen, pressing very hard.
Remove the paper pattern and draw decoration freehand onto the foil, again pressing very hard. This makes an embossed effect when the finished ornament is turned over.
Cut out the design and put a hole at the top. Attach a string for hanging.

MISTLETOE KISSING RING

You will need: 2 metal clothes-hangers, 2 wire hoops, (or enough wire to make 2 rings at least 20 cm in diameter), green crepe paper or tape, very thin wire, pieces of evergreens, mistletoe, ribbon.

Cover the rings with green tape or crepe paper. Fix them together at right angles with tape or wire. Using thin wire, attach bits of evergreen to the rings. Attach some mistletoe to the bottom. Decorate with red ribbon. Put a ribbon at the top for hanging. You can also hang small apples or little ornaments inside the rings.

CHRISTMAS CARD

You will need: coloured paper 20 cm x 15 cm, paper in a contrasting colour 5 cm x 15 cm, scissors, thin cardboard 5 cm x 15 cm to make a pattern.
Make a cardboard pattern of one half of a Christmas tree, as shown.
Place pattern on the small piece of coloured paper, draw around it and cut out carefully.
Fold the large coloured paper in half like a Christmas card.
Glue the "positive" and "negative" Christmas tree halves to the front as shown.
Write your Christmas greeting on the inside.
Experiment with other simple symmetrical shapes (bell, heart, star, etc.).

PAPER CHAINS

You will need: coloured paper, scissors.
Cut paper into strips about 10 cm wide and as long as you like. Cut slits in the paper first in one direction, then in the other as shown. Pull the ends apart with a twist.

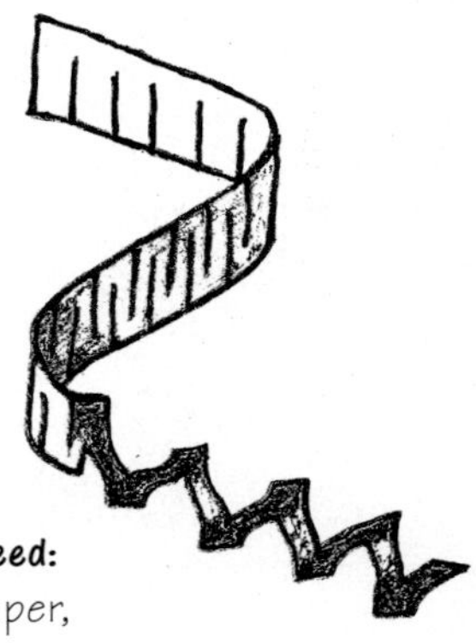

You will need: crepe paper, scissors.
Cut a long strip about 5 cm wide from a packet of crepe paper. Fold strip like an accordion. Cut out a pattern on each edge. Unfold the strip and twist it.

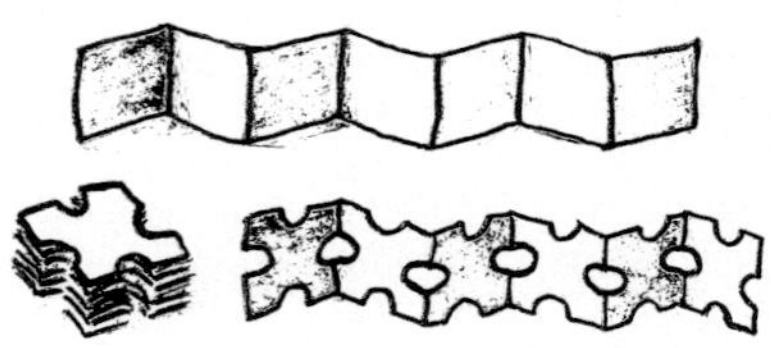

decorations

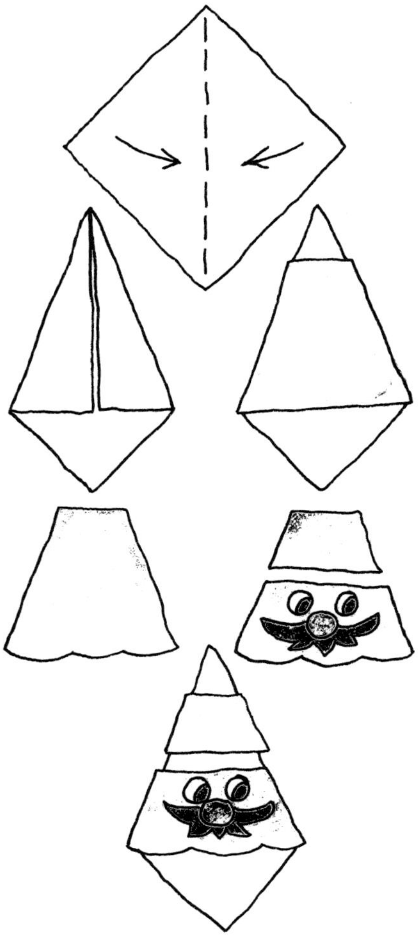

SANTA NAPKIN HOLDER

You will need: 2 pieces of red felt about 20 cm x 20 cm, small pieces of white and green felt, needle and thread, glue, white paper napkin.
Fold the napkin like a kite.
Put it on a piece of paper and draw around it to make a paper pattern.
Make the pattern 1 cm larger on each side than the napkin. Cut off about 6 cm from the top and make three "waves" at the widest part of the bottom as shown.
Use the pattern to cut two pieces of felt in that shape. Then on one of the pieces cut out a strip about 1 1/2 cm wide. Sew the three pieces together as shown. Be sure the top and bottom are even. There will be a hole in the front for some white napkin to show through – the fur of Santa's cap.
Cut out a moustache, nose and eyes from white, red and green felt. Glue them to Santa's face.
Put the white napkin inside. The top point of the napkin is Santa's cap, the bottom part is his beard.
If you like, make enough Santas for everyone at your Christmas dinner table.

CHRISTMAS STOCKING

You will need: 2 pieces of felt about 30 cm x 30 cm each, small pieces of felt in different colours, needle and thread, glue, scissors.
Make a paper pattern in the shape of a Christmas stocking. Be sure it is quite wide so that there is enough room in your stocking!
Use your pattern to cut out two stocking shapes from the felt. Sew them together leaving the top open.
Cut out Christmas designs, the letters of your name, or whatever you like from the other felt. Glue the felt pieces to your stocking. You could also sew on buttons, beads, sequins, bits of lace, etc.
Cut a strip of felt about 15 cm long and sew a loop to the top of the stocking so you can hang it up.
Maybe Santa will find your house

or your classroom

and put a surprise in your stocking!

DREAM CATCHERS

American Indians made these to keep away evil spirits, but today they are often used as Christmas tree decorations.
You will need: 2 sticks or straws about 10–15 cm long, yarn in different colours.
Tie the sticks together securely to form a cross. Beginning at the centre, put a piece of yarn over one stick and completely around it. Then do the same with the next stick. Keep going around, changing colours as you like. Leave about 1 cm at the end of each stick. Tie securely and make a yarn loop to hang it by.

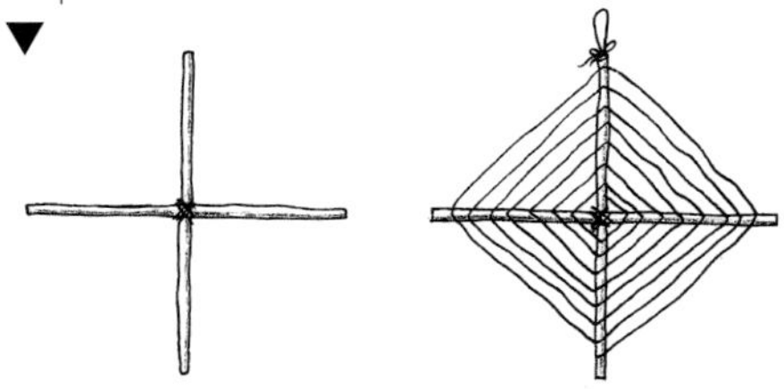

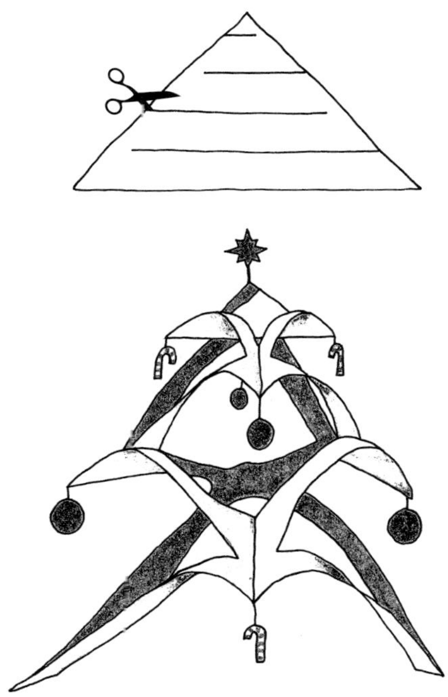

CHRISTMAS TREE MOBILE

You will need: a square of green paper or, preferably, thin cardboard (any size you like), bits of coloured paper, scissors, thread, glue.
Fold the square of paper in half diagonally, then fold it again. Cut alternately from two sides of the triangle, as shown, making at least three cuts in each direction. Unfold it carefully so that it is a square again. Lift up the middle. Cut out little ornaments from coloured paper. Glue a piece of thread to them and attach to the corners of the tree.
Tie some thread to the top of the mobile to hang it up.

A Taste of Christmas

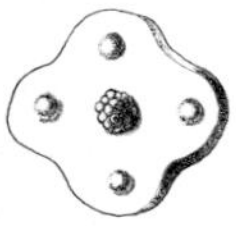

BROWNIES

150 g butter or margarine
400 g sugar
60 g cocoa
3 eggs
150 g flour
2 teaspoons vanilla flavouring or
2 packets vanilla sugar
pinch of salt
100 g chopped walnuts, if desired

Mix butter and sugar with an electric beater until smooth. Add other ingredients. The dough will be very thick. Spread it evenly into a greased 25 cm x 35 cm baking pan. Bake for 30 to 35 minutes at 160 °C. Cut into squares about 5 cm x 5 cm while still warm.

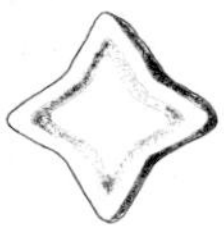

CHOCOLATE CHIP COOKIES

200 g butter or margarine
150 g sugar
150 g brown sugar
1 teaspoon vanilla flavouring or
1 packet vanilla sugar
2 eggs
350 g flour
1 teaspoon baking soda
1 teaspoon salt
1 12 oz package chocolate chips or
2 100g semi-sweet chocolate bars chopped into pea-size pieces
100 g chopped walnuts, if desired

Mix butter, sugars and vanilla until smooth. Beat in eggs, then flour, salt and baking soda. Stir in chocolate bits and nuts. Drop rounded teaspoonfuls of dough in little piles about 5 cm apart on a baking sheet (they spread when baked). Bake at 190 °C for 9–11 minutes until lightly browned.

GINGERBREAD MEN

50 g brown sugar
100 g butter or margarine
200 g treacle (AE molasses)
1 egg
420 g flour
1 tablespoon baking powder
1 teaspoon ground ginger
1 teaspoon ground cinnamon
1/2 teaspoon salt

Mix butter and sugar until smooth. Add other ingredients and mix well. Chill at least 2 hours. Take 1/4 of the dough at a time and leave the rest in the refrigerator. Roll it out and cut out desired shapes – people or hearts, stars, etc. Press raisins, nuts or bits of candied cherry into the dough for eyes, buttons, etc. Place on a greased baking sheet and bake at 180 °C about 8–10 minutes.
If desired, decorate with icing.

ICING

Mix 250 g powdered sugar and 1 tablespoon water. Add more water one spoon at a time until the icing can be spread easily. To make designs, put icing into an envelope and snip off a little bit of one corner. Squeeze the envelope carefully and "draw" with the icing.

SCOTTISH SHORTBREAD

225 g butter (not margarine!)
100 g sugar
280 g flour
pinch of salt

Mix butter and sugar until smooth. Add flour and salt. Roll out in a circle about 1 cm thick on a baking sheet or cut out small circles and place on a baking sheet. Prick the dough with a fork to make designs. Bake at 180 °C for about 20 minutes, until light brown and firm. Remove from baking sheet immediately.

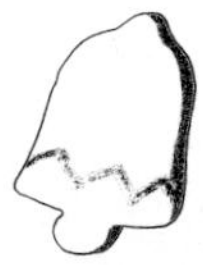

SNOWBALLS

225 g butter or margarine
70 g sugar
2 teaspoons water
2 teaspoons vanilla flavouring or
2 packets vanilla sugar
280 g flour
100 g chopped walnuts
powdered sugar (for rolling)

Mix butter and sugar until smooth. Add other ingredients except powdered sugar. Chill at least 4 hours. Roll into walnut-size balls. Place on ungreased baking sheet. Bake at 160 °C about 20 minutes. Cool slightly, then roll in powdered sugar.

dough [dəʊ] – Teig ***greased*** – eingefettet ***baking soda*** – Natron ***semi-sweet*** – halbbitter ***rounded*** – gehäuft ***pile*** – Häufchen ***treacle, molasses*** – Zuckerrübensirup ***ground*** – gemahlen ***ginger*** – Ingwer ***cinnamon*** – Zimt

A Taste of Christmas

TURKEY WITH SAGE AND ONION STUFFING

This is one way to roast a turkey: If using a frozen turkey, let it thaw first. Wash and stuff it (see recipe below). Put it in a large roasting pan, breast-side down and roast in the oven for one hour at 150 °C. Then turn the oven down to 85 °C. Roast the turkey for as many hours as pounds it weighs. For example, a 5-pound turkey (approx. 2500 g) takes 6 hours – one hour at 150 °C and five hours at the lower temperature.

Stuffing

200 g butter or margarine
3/4 cup chopped onion
1 1/2 cups chopped celery (stalks and leaves)
9 cups bread cubes made from white bread or
6 cups breadcrumbs
2 teaspoons salt
1 1/2 teaspoons ground sage
1 teaspoon dried thyme
1/2 teaspoon pepper

In a large pan, cook the onion and celery in the butter until the onion is soft. Add the other ingredients and stir. Put the stuffing into the turkey just before you are ready to roast it. Don't pack it in too tightly. If it doesn't all fit, you can put it around the sides of the roasting pan next to the turkey. If you do this, put some aluminum foil over it so it doesn't get too dry or burnt.

EGG NOG

6 eggs
1 cup sugar
1/2 teaspoon salt
rum flavouring, as much as desired
1 litre milk or part milk, part cream
nutmeg

Beat eggs until light and foamy. Add sugar and salt. Beat until thick. Add milk or cream. Chill at least 3 hours. Just before serving, sprinkle with nutmeg.

AUSTRALIAN CHRISTMAS PUDDING ICE CREAM

Since it is usually hot in Australia at Christmastime, many people there prefer to eat their Christmas pudding ice cold. There is no right or wrong way to make it. Take vanilla ice cream, let it get a little soft. Add raisins, nuts, dried fruit, glacé cherries, orange peel, cinnamon, rum flavouring – whatever you like. Line a pudding bowl with foil, put the ice cream in and freeze until hard. When ready to serve, turn it onto a plate and decorate with more nuts and fruit or a bit of holly.

WASSAIL HOT APPLE PUNCH

4 litres apple juice
1 teaspoon whole cloves
1 teaspoon whole allspice
2 cinnamon sticks

Heat juice and spices for 20 minutes, but do not boil.
Strain punch before serving.

CRANBERRY WALDORF SALAD

Waldorf salad was first created at the Waldorf Astoria Hotel in New York. This Christmassy version adds fresh cranberries and cinnamon to the more traditional ingredients.

1 1/2 cups fresh cranberries, chopped
2 red apples, chopped and with peel left on
3 sticks of celery, chopped
1 cup green seedless grapes, cut in half
1/3 cup raisins, if desired
1/4 cup walnuts, chopped

Dressing

250 g sour cream or joghurt
(or part mayonnaise, if desired)
1 teaspoon sugar
1 packet vanilla sugar or
1/2 teaspoon vanilla flavouring
1/4 teaspoon cinnamon

Mix the dressing ingredients until smooth. Add to the fruit and nuts. Cover and chill for 2 hours before serving.

to roast – braten (im Ofen) ***celery*** – Stangensellerie ***sage*** – Salbei ***stalk*** – Stange ***cube*** – Würfel ***cloves*** – Nelken ***allspice*** – Piment ***to boil*** – kochen ***to strain*** – sieben ***nutmeg*** – Muskat ***foamy*** – schaumig ***peel*** – Schale ***seedless*** – kernlos

Mince Pies & Christmas Pudding

If you ask an English person to name a typical Christmas speciality, the answer will nearly always be MINCE PIES! These are little pies filled with raisins, apples and spices. Most people buy the filling ready-made in jars, but it's possible to make it yourself too (see recipe below). In the old days there was also minced meat inside. In the Middle Ages the pies were baked in an oval shape with a pastry "baby" that symbolized the baby Jesus in the manger.

Pastry

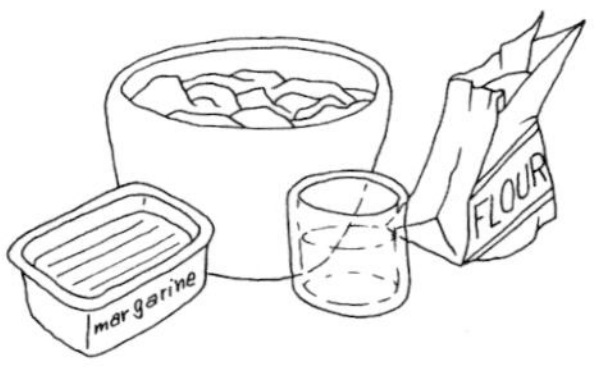

200 g flour
100 g margarine
pinch of salt
2 tablespoons cold water, or a little more

With your fingers, mix flour, margarine and salt until it looks like fine breadcrumbs.
Add enough water to make a smooth dough.

On a floured board, roll out the pastry.
With a glass, cut out circles about 6 cm and 8 cm in diameter.
Put the larger circles in a greased baking tray.

Put some mincemeat on the circle, then put a smaller pastry circle on top, sticking it to the bottom one.
Prick with a fork for steam to escape.
Bake at 200 °C for 30 minutes.
Sprinkle some sugar on top before serving.

The best-known of all English Christmas specialities is rather complicated to make. Lots of British people today don't make their own Christmas puddings, but buy them at the supermarket.

Of those who do make them themselves, every family has their own recipe and often their own ceremony for making the pudding – stirring a special way, making a wish, adding coins for good luck, etc. This is a version which uses margarine instead of the more traditional suet.

150 g flour
2 teaspoons mixed spice (or use a mixture of cinnamon, cloves and ginger)
1 teaspoon nutmeg
85 g fresh white breadcrumbs
100 g margarine
100 g raisins
200 g currants
200 g sultanas
100 g chopped apple
75 g brown sugar
grated rind of 1 lemon
2 eggs, beaten
2 tablespoons brandy or rum

Mix all ingredients in the order given. Make a wish and stir once more. Put into a greased pudding basin, cover with foil. Set in a pressure cooker with water half-way up the basin and cook for 2 hours OR put the pudding in a large pan of water and bake in the oven for 8 hours, adding water when necessary.

When pudding is cold, cover with fresh foil and store in a cool place, for several weeks if possible. Before serving, heat it again either in a pressure cooker for 30 to 45 minutes or in the oven or microwave until it is hot.

Decorate the top with holly leaves. Serve with brandy butter.

Mincemeat

225 g raisins
225 g currants
225 g sultanas
225 g brown sugar
125 g chopped candied lemon and orange peel
675 g apples, peeled and chopped
1 lemon, juice and rind, grated
1 teaspoon nutmeg
1 wineglass of brandy

Mix all ingredients. Stir well, cover and leave overnight. Stir again the next day. Put into dry jars and cover as for jam, or freeze until ready to use. It's best to wait at least two weeks before using so the flavours can blend.

Hurrah for the pudding

Brandy Butter

75 g butter
75 g sugar
2 tablespoons brandy

Beat the butter until creamy. Slowly add the sugar.

Add the brandy a drop at a time.

minced – gehackt ***pastry*** – Teig ***currant*** – Korinthe ***suet*** – Talg ***basin*** – Schüssel ***pressure cooker*** – Dampfkochtopf

MERRY QUIZMAS

1. What do most British people eat for Christmas dinner?
A) fish and chips
B) roast beef
C) turkey

2. The Christmas tree was made popular in Britain by
A) one of Henry VIII's wives
B) Queen Victoria's husband
C) a German cousin of Queen Elizabeth I

3. Who speaks on TV every December 25 at 3 pm?
A) The Prime Minister
B) The Queen
C) The Archbishop of Canterbury

4. What do British people do with Christmas crackers?
A) eat them with cheese
B) pull them apart and find a gift inside
C) watch them explode in the sky on Christmas Eve

5. Which country sends a large Christmas tree to Trafalgar Square in London every year?
A) Norway
B) Germany
C) Sweden

6. What is often hidden in an English Christmas pudding?
A) five gold rings
B) coins
C) three silver buttons

7. What bird is seen most often on English Christmas cards?
A) a wren
B) an early bird
C) a robin

8. When he is not delivering presents, Santa Claus lives
A) on an island in the Caribbean
B) at the North Pole
C) in the Norwegian woods

9. In Britain December 26 is known as
A) Boxing Day
B) St Stephen's Day
C) St Patrick's Day

10. Which Christmas song has sold more recordings than any other?
A) Elvis Presley singing "Silent Night"
B) Bing Crosby singing "White Christmas"
C) Michael Jackson singing "Jingle Bells"

At least 20 words are hidden in this puzzle. Most of them are mentioned in the quiz. How many can you find?

W	N	H	C	A	Y	A	D	G	N	I	X	O	B
U	O	O	C	R	A	C	K	E	R	S	A	K	M
T	R	N	B	E	V	I	C	S	N	E	E	U	Q
S	T	A	R	R	I	E	A	N	O	R	W	A	Y
W	H	I	T	E	C	H	R	I	S	T	M	A	S
D	P	K	G	R	T	O	O	O	Y	U	L	E	O
R	O	B	I	N	O	L	L	G	T	R	E	E	N
A	L	N	F	R	R	L	S	S	I	K	L	E	G
G	E	S	T	L	I	Y	K	T	N	E	R	W	N
O	S	A	N	T	A	M	E	R	R	Y	R	A	N

THE SNOWMAN

by Mabel Marlowe

A snowman once stood upon a hill, with his face towards the sunset. A very fine snowman he was, as tall as a soldier, and much fatter. He had two pieces of glass for eyes, and a stone for a nose, and a piece of black wood for a mouth, and in his hand he held a stout, knobbly club.

But he had no clothes at all, not even a hat, and the wind on the top of that hill was as bitter as wind could be.

"How cold I am! I am as cold as ice!" said the snowman. "But that red sky looks warm." So he lifted his feet from the ground, and went tramp, tramp, tramping down the slope towards the setting sun.

Very soon he overtook a gipsy woman, who was wearing a bright red shawl. "Ha, that looks warm! I must have it," thought the snowman. So he went up to the gipsy woman and he said, "Give me that red shawl."

"No indeed! I cannot spare it on this wintry day," answered the gipsy. "I am cold enough as it is."

"Cold!" shouted the snowman in a very growlish voice. "Are you as cold as I am, I wonder! Are you cold inside as well as outside? Are you made of ice, through and through and through?"

"No, I suppose not," mumbled the gipsy, who was getting hot with fright.

"Then give me your red shawl this moment, or I shall strike you with my stout, knobbly club."

Then the gipsy took off her red shawl, grumbling all the time, and gave it to the snowman. He put it round his shoulders, without a word of thanks, and went tramp, tramp tramping down the hill. And the shivering gipsy followed behind him.

Presently the snowman overtook a milkmaid who was wearing her grandmother's long red woollen mittens.

"Ha, they look warm! I must have them," thought the snowman. So he went up to the milkmaid and he said, "Give me those red woollen mittens."

"No, indeed!" said the milkmaid. "They belong to my grandmother. She lent them to me because my fingers were so cold."

"Cold!" shouted the Snowman, in a very roarish voice. "Are your fingers as cold as mine, I wonder! Are your hands and arms frozen into ice, through and through and through?"

"No, I suppose not," mumbled the milkmaid.

"Then give me those red mittens, this moment, or I shall strike you with my stout, knobbly club."

So the milkmaid took off the warm mittens, grumbling all the time, and the snowman put them on, without a word of thanks. Then he went tramp, tramp, tramping down the hill. And the gipsy and the milkmaid followed him.

After a while he overtook a pirate wearing a pirate's thick red cap, with a tassel dangling down his back.

"Ha! That looks warm! I must have it," said the snowman. So he went up to the pirate and he said, "Give me that red tassel cap."

"No indeed!" said the pirate. "A nice cold in the head I should get if I did."

"Cold in the head!" shouted the snowman, in a very thunderish voice. "Is your head as cold as mine, I wonder! Are your brains made of snow, and your bones solid ice, through and through and through?"

"No, I suppose not," muttered the pirate.

"Then give me that red tassel cap, this moment, or I shall set upon you with my stout, knobbly club."

Now the pirate felt very sorry that he had turned tame, but he did not like the look of that knobbly stick, so he gave up his red tassel cap. The snowman put it on without a word of thanks. Then he went tramp, tramp, tramping down the hill, with the tassel bumping up and down. And the gipsy woman, and the milkmaid, and the pirate followed him.

At last he reached the bottom of the hill, where the village school house stood, and there was the village schoolmaster on the doorstep, looking at the sunset. He was smoking a pipe, and on his feet were two red velvet slippers.

"Ha, those look warm! I must have them," said the snowman. So he went up to the schoolmaster and said, "Give me those red slippers."

"Certainly, if you want them," said the schoolmaster. "Take them by all means. It is far too cold today to be tramping about with bare toes," and he stooped and took off his slippers, and there he stood in some bright red socks, thick and woolly and knitted by hand.

"Ha! Those socks look warm! Give them to me," said the snowman.

"Certainly, if you want them," said the schoolmaster. "But you must come inside. I cannot take my socks off here in the doorway. Come onto the mat."

So the snowman stepped into the doorway, and stood upon the mat.

"Be sharp with those socks. My feet are as cold as solid ice," he grumbled.

"I am sorry to hear that," said the schoolmaster. "But I have a warm red blanket airing over the stove. Come in, sir. Sit on that chair by the fire, sir. Put your cold feet upon this snug red footstool, and let me wrap this red blanket around your legs."

So the snowman came into the schoolhouse, and sat upon a chair by the glowing fire, and put his feet upon the red footstool, and the schoolmaster wrapped the red blanket round and round and round his legs. (And all this while the gipsy woman, and the milkmaid, and the pirate were peering in at the window.)

"Are you feeling warmer?" asked the schoolmaster.

"No, I am as cold as an iceberg."

"Come closer to the fire."

So the schoolmaster pushed the chair closer to the fire, but the snowman gave him not one word of thanks.

"Are you feeling warmer now?"

"No, I am as cold as a stone. My feet feel like icy water."

"Move closer to the fire," said the schoolmaster, and he pushed the chair right against the kerb. "There! Are you warmer now?"

"No, no, no! I am colder than ever. I cannot feel my feet at all. I cannot feel my legs at all. I cannot feel my back at all."

Then the schoolmaster pushed the chair quite close up against the stove. "Are you warmer now?"

But there was no answer, except a slithery sliding sound, and the drip, drip, drip of black snow-water.

"Dear me!" whispered the snowman, in a gurgling kind of voice. "I have dropped my stout, knobbly club. My red slippers are floating into the ashpan. My mittens are swimming in a little river on the floor. My shawl is gone. My red tassel cap is slipping – slipping away. My head is going … going …

Splosh! Splash! Gurgle!

"That's the end of him," said the schoolmaster, and he went to fetch the mop.

Then the gipsy woman, and the milkmaid, and the pirate came in and picked up their things, and wrung them out, and dried them at the stove, and the schoolmaster put his red slippers on the hearth, and hung the red blanket over the back of the chair.

Then he picked up the stout, knobbly club and gave the fire a poke.

stout, knobbly club – kräftiger, knorriger Knüppel ***gipsy*** – Zigeuner(in) ***slope*** – Gefälle ***to overtake*** – überholen ***to spare*** – entbehren ***to shiver*** – zittern ***tassel*** – Bommel ***velvet*** – Samt ***by all means*** – selbstverständlich ***hearth*** – [hɑːθ] Feuerstelle ***poke*** – Stoß ***chubby*** – *a bit fat*

CHUBBY LITTLE SNOWMAN

A chubby little snowman
Had a carrot nose.
Along came a bunny,
And what do you suppose?
That hungry little bunny,
Looking for his lunch,
Ate the snowman's carrot nose,
Nibble, nibble, crunch!

Anon.

THE CREMATION

by Robert W. Service

There are strange things done in the midnight sun
By the men who moil for gold;
The Arctic trails have their secret tales
That would make your blood run cold;
The northern lights have seen queer sights,
But the queerest they ever did see
Was that night on the marge of Lake Lebarge
I cremated Sam McGee.

Now Sam McGee was from Tennessee, where the cotton blooms and blows.
Why he left his home in the South to roam 'round the pole, God only knows.
He was always cold, but the land of gold seemed to hold him like a spell,
Though he'd often say in his homely way that he'd "sooner live in hell."

On Christmas Day we were mushing our way over the Dawson Trail.
Talk of your cold! Through the parka's fold it stabbed like a driven nail.
If our eyes we'd close, then the lashes froze till sometimes we couldn't see;
It wasn't much fun, but the only one to whimper was Sam McGee.

And that very night, as we lay packed tight in our robes beneath the snow,
And the dogs were fed, and the stars o'erhead were dancing heel and toe,
He turned to me, and "Cap," says he, "I'll cash in this trip, I guess,
And if I do, I'm asking you that you won't refuse my last request."

Well, he seemed so low that I couldn't say no; then he says with a sort of moan;
"It's the cursed cold, and it's got right hold till I'm chilled clean through to the bone.
Yet 'taint being dead – it's my awful dread of the icy grave that pains.
So I want you to swear that, foul or fair, you'll cremate my last remains."

A pal's last need is a thing to heed, so I swore I would not fail;
And we started on at the streak of dawn; but God! he looked ghastly pale.
He crouched on the sleigh, and he raved all day of his home in Tennessee;
And before nightfall a corpse was all that was left of Sam McGee.

There wasn't a breath in that land of death, and I hurried, horror-driven,
With a corpse half hid that I couldn't get rid, because of a promise I'd given;
It was lashed to the sleigh, and it seemed to say, "You may tax your brawn and brains,
But you promised true, and it's up to you to cremate those last remains."

Now a promise made is a debt unpaid, and the trail has its own stern code;
In the days to come, though my lips were dumb, in my heart how I cursed that load.
In the long, long night, by the lone firelight, while the huskies, 'round in a ring,
Howled out their woes to the homeless snows – O God! how I loathed the thing.

And every day that quiet clay seemed to heavy and heavier grow;
And on I went, though the dogs were spent and the grub was getting low;
The trail was bad, and I felt half mad, but I swore I would not give in;
And I'd often sing to the hateful thing, and it harkened with a grin.

Till I came to the marge of Lake Lebarge, and a derelict there lay;
It was jammed in the ice, but I saw in a trice it was called the "Alice May".
And I looked at it, and I thought a bit, and I looked at my frozen chum;
Then "Here," said I, with a sudden cry, "is my cre-ma-tor-i-um."

OF SAM McGEE

Some planks I tore from the cabin floor, and I lit the boiler fire;
Some coal I found that was lying around, and I heaped the fuel higher;
The flames just soared, and the furnace roared – such a blaze you seldom see;
And I burrowed a hole in the glowing coal, and I stuffed in Sam McGee.

Then I made a hike, for I didn't like to hear him sizzle so;
And the heavens scowled, and the huskies howled, and the wind began to blow.
It was icy cold, but the hot sweat rolled down my cheeks, and I don't know why;
And the greasy smoke in an inky cloak went streaking down the sky.

I do not know how long in the snow I wrestled with grisly fear;
But the stars came out and they danced about ere again I ventured near;
I was sick with dread, but I bravely said: "I'll just take a peep inside.
I guess he's cooked, and it's time I looked;" ... then the door I opened wide.

And there sat Sam, looking cold and calm, in the heart of the furnace roar;
And he wore a smile you could see a mile, and he said: "Please close that door!
It's fine in here, but I greatly fear you'll let in the cold and storm –
Since I left Plumtree down in Tennessee, it's the first time I've been warm."

There are strange things done in the midnight sun
By the men who moil for gold;
The Arctic trails have their secret tales
That would make your blood run cold;
The northern lights have seen queer sights,
But the queerest they ever did see
Was that night on the marge of Lake Lebarge
I cremated Sam McGee.

DISCUSSION QUESTIONS

1. Do you remember a time in your life when you felt extremely cold? When was it?
2. If you could choose, would you like to live in a place with very cold winters? Why or why not?
3. How do extremes in temperature or climate influence people's behaviour?
4. Have you ever made a promise to a friend that was very difficult to keep? What did you do?
5. If you had lived during the time of the gold rush in the Yukon or in California, would you have left your home or even your country to go and look for gold? Why do you think so many people did so?

cremation – *burning of a dead body* ***to moil*** – *to work very hard* ***marge*** – *edge* ***spell*** – Zauber ***to mush*** – *to travel with a dog sled* ***to whimper*** – *to cry weakly* ***o'erhead*** – *(poet) overhead, above us* ***Cap*** – *short for Captain* ***to cash in*** – *(sl) to die (from poker, when one leaves the game and exchanges chips for money won or lost)* ***clean*** – *completely* ***'taint*** = *it ain't – it isn't* ***to heed*** – beachten ***pale*** – blass ***to rave*** – *to talk wildly* ***corpse*** – *dead body* ***to tax*** – strapazieren ***brawn*** – *strength* ***stern*** – streng ***code*** – *set of rules* ***husky*** – Schlittenhund ***woe*** – Sorge ***to loathe*** – *to hate* ***clay*** – Lehm (*here: the body*) ***grub*** – *food* ***to harken*** – *to listen* ***derelict*** – verlassenes Boot ***in a trice*** – *quickly* ***chum*** – *friend* ***hike*** – Spaziergang ***to sizzle*** – brutzeln ***to scowl*** – *to look angry* ***inky*** – *very dark* ***cloak*** – *coat, cover* ***ere*** – *before* ***to venture*** – sich trauen

JINGLE BELL ROCK

Words and music J. Beal and J. Boothe

JINGLE BELLS

Words and music J. Pierpont (1785–1866)

A day or two ago
I thought I'd take a ride,
Soon Miss Fanny Bright
was seated by my side,
The horse was lean and lank,
Misfortune seemed his lot,
He got into a drifted bank,
and we, we got "upsot"!

FIND THE DIFFERENCES

Work with a partner. One of you has picture A, the other has picture B.

Poems Poems Poems

WINTER DAYS

Biting air
Winds blow
City streets
Under snow

Noses red
Lips sore
Runny eyes
Hands raw

Chimneys smoke
Cars crawl
Piled snow
On garden wall

Slush in gutters
Ice in lanes
Frosty patterns
On window panes

Morning call
Lift up head
Nipped by winter
Stay in bed.

Gareth Owen

IT'S CHRISTMAS

It's Christmas! Merry Christmas!
Yes, it's merry, merry Christmas,
it's a time for hanging stockings,
it's a time for riding sleighs,
it's a time for jolly greeting,
snow and holly, overeating,
oh, I love you merry Christmas,
you're the best of holidays.

Jack Prelutsky

SNOW TOWARD EVENING

Suddenly the sky turned grey,
The day,
Which had been bitter and chill,
Grew soft and still.
Quietly
From some invisible blossoming tree
Millions of petals cool and white
Drifted and blew,
Lifted and flew,
Fell with the falling night.

Melville Cane

STOPPING BY WOODS ON A SNOWY EVENING

Whose woods these are I think I know,
His house is in the village though;
He will not see me stopping here
To watch his woods fill up with snow.

My little horse must think it queer
To stop without a farmhouse near
Between the woods and frozen lake
The darkest evening of the year.

He gives his harness bells a shake
To ask if there is some mistake.
The only other sound's the sweep
Of easy wind and downy flake.

The woods are lovely, dark and deep,
But I have promises to keep,
And miles to go before I sleep,
And miles to go before I sleep.

Robert Frost

THE BELLS

Hear the sledges with the bells –
Silver bells!
What a world of merriment their melody foretells!
How they tinkle, tinkle, tinkle,
In the icy air of night!
While the stars that oversprinkle
All the heavens seem to twinkle
With a crystalline delight;
Keeping time, time, time,
In a sort of Runic rhyme,
To the tintinnabulation that so musically wells
From the bells, bells, bells, bells,
Bells, bells, bells –
From the jingling and the tinkling of the bells.

Edgar Allan Poe

WINTER MORNING

Winter is the king of showmen,
Turning tree stumps into snowmen
And houses into birthday cakes
And spreading sugar over lakes.
Smooth and clean and frosty white,
The world looks good enough to bite.
That's the season to be young,
Catching snowflakes on your tongue.

Snow is snowy when it's snowing,
I'm sorry it's slushy when it's going.

Ogden Nash

EVERYWHERE, CHRISTMAS TONIGHT

Everywhere – everywhere, Christmas tonight!
Christmas in lands of the fir tree and pine,
Christmas in lands of the palm tree and vine,
Christmas where snow peaks stand solemn and white,
Christmas where cornfields lie sunny and bright.
Everywhere, everywhere, Christmas tonight!

Phillips Brooks

CHRISTMAS JOY

Somehow, not only for Christmas
But all the long year through,
The joy that you give to others
Is the joy that comes back to you.

John Greenleaf Whittier

TEACHER'S NOTES

The texts and activities in *Merry Christmas* have been selected and written to be as flexible as possible and adaptable to a wide range of age and language levels. You the teacher can best decide which items would be most enjoyable and suitable for you and your classes.

The material is organized by theme rather than language level. While Christmas in the English-speaking world is the overall topic, many activities are multi-cultural in approach and the materials can be used with students from cultures that do not celebrate Christmas.

Vocabulary aids have been kept to a minimum and are limited to words which could probably not be easily guessed from the context or which might not be found in small dictionaries.

TEACHING SUGGESTIONS – ANSWERS TO THE PUZZLES

3

Christmas Wish

To every hearth a little fire,
To every board a little feast,
To every heart a joy,
To every child a toy,
Shelter for bird and beast.

5

Season's Greeetings around the World

The purpose of this activity isn't to find out how many of the languages students can recognize, but to expose them to a wide range of "strange" languages and writing systems. This in itself can be fascinating and can help students realize that while not everyone in the world celebrates Christmas, every culture has some kind of winter or New Year's festival and some kind of special greeting for it.

This activity can be used at any language or age level, either cut apart as *dominoes* as described on the student's page or left uncut, as a matching and discussion activity. It's best if students work on it in pairs or groups of three.

Students may enjoy comparing the languages and telling what they know about them as well as telling the class how to say "Merry Christmas" or "Happy New Year" in other languages they know.

Note on some of the languages:

Afrikaans, spoken in parts of South Africa, developed from 17th century Dutch. **Gujarati** is an Indo-Aryan language spoken in western India. **Hawaiian** *Mele Kalikimaka* is really the English *Merry Christmas* but since Hawaiian uses only twelve letters and no consonant clusters, that is what happens to it. The **Hebrew** shown here is the modern version used in present-day Israel. **Northern Sotho** is spoken in parts of southern Africa. **Serbo-Croatian**: While the languages of the Serbs and the Croats are nearly identical, the Roman Catholic Croats use the Latin alphabet while the Orthodox Serbs usually use the Cyrillic one.

Most of the expressions mean literally either Happy or Good Christmas. Hebrew, Gujarati, Russian, Chinese and Persian are New Year's greetings or general holiday greetings.

Additional activities:
Make a class collage of Christmas or New Year's greetings in lots of different languages. Encourage students in your class who are from different cultures to tell about the special days they celebrate and the greetings they use. Some students could also interview people from other cultures about how they celebrate special days.

6/7

Celebrating the Season

Discussion questions:
If you had to choose from among the six places, where would you prefer to spend Christmas? Why? Which description is most similar/most different from the way you celebrate in your family?

Writing activity:
Write a similar report (perhaps in letter form) about how you celebrate Christmas or New Year (or another special day) in your family or your town.

8

Hanukkah

See also the report by Elliott Green (p. 6) and *Christmas dictionary* (p. 79).

10/11

Adrian Mole's Christmas

Depending on the level of trust within the class, students could share experiences they have had with keeping diaries and/or talk about why some people write in diaries. Students might be inspired to write a fictional or semi-autobiographical Christmas story of their own in diary form.

12

An English Christmas Dinner

Who is sitting where?

Jack Julie Jenny
Jane Jason
John Jill James

Have students write a menu of a favourite or typical festive menu in their family and then compare the menus with their classmates. In small groups, plan ideal menus for meals at Christmastime.

Christmas Dinner Word Find

W	A	G	B	I	M	E	V	H	I	C
R	O	N	I	O	N	W	D	B	G	E
G	N	I	F	F	U	T	S	T	N	G
E	Y	D	N	A	R	B	H	U	Y	A
S	D	D	C	S	T	U	O	R	P	S
F	F	U	Q	G	P	K	J	K	O	E
X	L	P	O	T	A	T	O	E	S	I
K	Z	U	A	G	R	A	V	Y	T	P

13

Christmas is Together Time

While some texts could arguably be suitable to several pictures, the cartoonist's texts are as follows:

1-H 2-A 3-L 4-G 5-J 6-B 7-E 8-D 9-K 10-C 11-F 12-I

Students might like to continue the activity with their own sentences (plus pictures?) beginning with "Christmas is ..." A classroom collage (poster or door decoration) could be made with the results.

14

Under the Mistletoe

The power of mistletoe is also a theme in *The Chime Child* (pp. 15–17). See also *The Story of Christmas* p. 19 and craft activity on p. 58. After reading the poem, students might try making up a story about what happened before and after the situation described in the poem. See also *robins* in *Christmas dictionary* p. 80.

15–17

The Chime Child

Telling ghost stories has long been part of the Christmas tradition in Britain. Charles Dickens wrote *A Christmas Carol* (see pp 20–23) in this tradition.

Mistletoe see above.

20

Charles Dickens's *A Christmas Carol*

There are several video and audio versions of the story, including one which is read by Patrick Stewart, known to many students as Captain Picard from *Star Trek* (Simon & Schuster Audio).

21–23

Ebenezer Scrooge

This short play introduces beginners to the characters and themes of the classic Dickens story. The scenes can be practised in small groups as they all involve different characters and provide a short role for a large number of students. Only Scrooge himself appears in each scene, so it may be necessary for different students to take his role. If the scenes are later presented as a play to an audience, the different Scrooges could wear a characteristic hat or sign.

The illustrations by Quentin Blake are from a series of British postage stamps issued on November 9, 1993 commemorating the 150th anniversary of the first edition of *A Christmas Carol.*

(See also *Charles Dickens: Scrooge*, by David Hilborne-Clarke, Cornelsen 1992, in the series *Plays for reading and acting.*)

25

The Christmas Spider

This story may remind your students of other Christmas legends about talking animals, special flowers that open at Christmas, etc. See also the robin legend on p. 14.

27–29

Christmas with the Herdmans

Much of the humour and charm of the Herdman story is based on the children's naive misunderstandings of the old biblical language. Perhaps your students have had similar problems with misunderstandings of old-fashioned words in stories or songs and could share their experiences.

Biblical quotations are from the King James translation of the Bible. See p. 30.

30

The Christmas Story According to Saint Luke

The King James translation is the traditional version that the mother reads to the children in *Christmas with the Herdmans* (pp. 27–29).

Students could listen to the text and pretend they were the Herdman children and had never heard the story before. Which words and expressions are unusual or could cause misunderstandings?

The King James Bible, also called the Authorized Version as it was the translation appointed to be read in churches throughout the kingdom, was first published in 1611, the year Shakespeare retired from writing. For several centuries no other single book had such an enormous influence on the English language. Numerous quotations and allusions from it are still used knowingly or unknowingly in literature and conversation.

Its language preserves old structures such as inverted word order rather than *do* forms in questions and negatives, *thee, thou* and *thy* for second person singular pronouns, and *ye* instead of *you* for the second person plural subject.

Since the 1960s an ever-increasing number of new Bible translations have been made and the Authorized Version is no longer the exclusive version read in Protestant churches. The 1989 translation in this book is a revised version of one first published in 1970 by a combined effort of Cambridge and Oxford University Press.

31

King's College Cambridge

Check a BBC guide to find out when you can hear this year's Service of Nine Lessons and Carols. If there is an English-language church in your area (check the phone book of larger cities), they may have a similar carol service in December.

Students could share their own experiences and feelings about singing a solo, playing an instrument, or reciting a poem in front of an audience.

32

Message to the Shepherds

PEN – N + BALL – BLL + CAKE – AK = PEACE
MONKEY – KEY – M = ON
BELL + CAR + TH – BLLC = EARTH

G R E A T J O Y
1 2 3 4 5 6 7 8

34

Rudolph and I Were Something Alike

This text as well as the information about *The Night Before Christmas* (p. 39) contribute to the insight that many so-called traditions were actually created by individual people for specific reasons. Rudolph and the other reindeer have not always been part of Christmas.

Although some may consider the Rudolph story just something for young children, this text presents a different aspect of the story which older students can appreciate, too.

35

One Foggy Christmas Eve ...

For a listening activity, cut the pictures apart and mix them up. Have students put the pictures in order as you read the story. Or in pairs: one person reads while the other arranges the pictures.

36–38

How the Grinch Stole Christmas

Like many of Dr. Seuss's words, *Grinch* can't be found in a dictionary. You could talk about sound symbolism and whether *grinch* sounds like something positive or negative. The strong rhythms of the "story-poem" make it ideal for reading aloud. Consider presenting it as a choral reading for an audience with parts of the poem read by small groups. Video and picture book versions of this story are also available.

39

The Night Before Christmas

see *Music in the Classroom* (p. 76).

40

Why Do We Deceive Our Children Each Christmas About Santa Claus?

Before reading the text, students can share their experiences about believing in Santa Claus, when and how they found out the truth, whether they think it's good or bad to tell children such "lies", and why children want to believe the stories and adults want to tell them. The text is from a book titled *Why Things Are: Answers to Every Essential Question in Life.*

What If There Really Was a Santa Claus?

Students could speculate on this question before reading the text and/or add their own ideas to the list after reading it.

42

Perfect Present

If you read the poem aloud, you could stop before the end of every other line and have students guess the rhyming word. Or white-out those words on the student's pages and have them guess the words. You could also block out the last words in every line (more difficult).

Introductory or follow-up project: Make up an imaginary pet. What can it do? What does it eat? Where does it live? Describe it and draw a picture of it.

Message to Santa

I'll fax you my complete list tomorrow.

Word search:
ponytail, beard, knee, boots, cap, coat, door, nose, child, mother

L	I	A	T	Y	N	O	P	C	A
B	D	U	C	A	C	Z	O	B	Y
W	N	O	S	E	A	M	X	E	W
O	M	Y	V	B	P	T	F	A	X
R	C	M	U	L	S	P	Q	R	K
R	D	O	E	C	H	I	L	D	N
O	E	T	L	I	S	T	R	M	E
M	E	H	H	'	I	A	O	N	E
O	F	E	G	L	B	O	O	T	S
T	J	R	?	L	!	C	D	O	R

43

Long Walk Part of Gift

Discussion starters: Make a list of three special gifts you have received and three you have given. Have you ever given/received a gift which was very special but which cost nothing or nearly nothing? What makes a gift special? Bring something to class which you once received as a gift and is special to you, even though it has little or no monetary value.

Giving

1 holly, 2 why, 3 evergreen, 4 toy, 5 foot,
6 shoot, 7 unusual, 8 wives, 9 bit, 10 giving,
11 style, 12 soft, 13 yes, 14 top, 15 is, 16 you,
17 UFO, 18 GI, 19 every, 20 I

You give but little when you give of your possessions. It is when you give of yourself that you truly give.

44

What's in the Packages?

elephant, drum, trumpet, hippopotamus, gum, porpoise, robot, brownies, dragon.

Christmas Thank-Yous

Have students look through old magazines or catalogues and cut out pictures of things that could be given as Christmas gifts, but that are as unusual or improbable as possible. Collect the pictures (you may need to censor them a bit) and the next day give each student one picture of a Christmas gift he or she supposedly received from an elderly aunt. Each student has to write a nice thank-you note to the aunt and express great appreciation for the gift but shouldn't mention it by name. The thank-you letters are then collected and mixed up and students have to guess which letter goes with which gift.

46/47

The Twelve Days of Christmas

See activities related to the song (pp. 76, 77).

Art project:
Have students choose one of the days and draw an illustration or cartoon for it. The class could make a series of 12 drawings and arrange them in a display.

48

The Gift of the Magi

Groups of three students could record this story as a radio play using sound effects.

49

Snowman, Snowflakes and Snowballs

1. CARD Christmas card, card game, postcard, cardboard, birthday card. 2. STAR filmstar, starfish, shooting star, starboard (Etymologically, starboard has nothing to do with stars, but is from an Old English word *steor*, a paddle or rudder, related to German *Steuer*), Star Trek (science fiction series on TV). 3. COLD cold feet (to get cold feet is to become afraid or very nervous), cold turkey (immediate stop to taking drugs), cold blood (*in cold blood* means to do sth especially cruelly or violently), cold war, cold front (in the weather report). 4. RED Red Cross, redhead (person with red hair), red tape (excessive bureaucracy or complicated paper work – Lawyers and government officials used to tie their documents and papers with red tape), red carpet (You roll out a red carpet when an important person comes. Note: In English, the expression *VIP* for *very important person* is pronounced 'vi:'ai'pi:), redwood (Redwood trees grow in northern California and southern Oregon. They can be 100 metres tall and over 2000 years old.) 5. LIGHT lightweight, highlight, lightbulb, lighthouse, light year. 6. BELL cowbell, bellflower (small, blue, bell-shaped flower), doorbell, bell bottoms (trousers that are wide at the bottom like sailors wear), bellboy (in a hotel). 7. GREEN greenhorn (inexperienced or naive person, newcomer – from a young animal with young or "green" horns), greenback (slang for an American dollar because the back is printed in green ink), Greenpeace (environmental organization founded in Canada in 1971), greenhouse (glass building where plants are grown indoors, cf. greenhouse effect, green belt (land around a city with fields and parks where people are not allowed to build houses or factories). 8. TREE Christmas tree, treetop, tree frog, tree house, family tree 9. ICE dry ice (solid carbon dioxide), Ice Age, ice cube, ice skate, ice cream.
Although even very advanced students probably won't know all of these expressions, the activity can still be done successfully with students beginning at a low intermediate level if they use their imagination and their dictionaries. It works best if students first try it in pairs or small groups so they can pool their ideas. After that phase, the whole class can work together and collectively they should be able to find most of the answers by thinking creatively. In fact, this type of exercise is typical for those used in creativity-training seminars.

What's That?

Father Christmas

Star Puzzle

Answers will vary. Any words can be accepted as long as the players can logically explain them and the others accept the explanation.
Words that have something to do with Christmas: turkey, toys, tinsel, Twelve Days of Christmas; angel, Advent, advertisements, reindeer, Rudolph, roof, robin ...

50/51

Picture and Word Cards

There are 18 word and definition cards and 24 picture cards. The six extra picture cards (*gingerbread man, snowman, stars, candle, bell, candy cane*) are given so that the pictures can be used for an Advent calendar.

The pictures alone can be used as an introduction to English Christmas customs. Words, definitions and pictures can be cut apart and matched together, possibly making a little booklet or poster.

Christmas Memory

(also called *Concentration*) In small groups, students take turns turning over two cards looking for pairs. If they find a pair, they get another turn. Pairs to be matched could be either words and pictures or pictures and definitions. Or try three-way memory using all three types of cards and students turning over three cards at a time looking for "triplets".

Bingo

Photocopy either one picture section (or one word section) per person in class plus one extra copy for the group leader(s). Each student prepares a bingo card by choosing 16 of the 18 pictures (or words) and gluing them in random order on a piece of paper in four rows of four items each. Each bingo card should be different. The group leader has a set of all 18 pictures, words or definitions. He or she reads one definition or shows one picture at a time. The student(s) who have the corresponding picture/text cover it on their card with a marker. It's best to use bits of coloured paper, buttons or coins for this rather than marking the boxes with a pencil. The first person with four items in a row covered – across, down or diagonally – says "Merry Christmas" and is the winner. The prize could be either a small Christmas sweet and/or the privilege of being the group leader for the next round. Be sure students remove all markers on their cards before the next round begins. This game can be played either as a whole class activity or in groups of 4–6.

To make the *Bingo* or *Memory* games more durable, either photocopy the pages on heavy paper or glue the pictures/texts to lightweight cardboard. They could also be laminated if your school has such a machine, or else covered on both sides with transparent sticky plastic. Students will probably want to colour the pictures before covering them in plastic. You may want to enlarge the cards for *Memory* games or else glue them to larger pieces of paper. A set of *Memory* cards or a *Bingo* game would make a nice gift, especially if put into a decorated box or envelope. Students might like to make a set for a friend or brother/sister or possibly as gifts to some charitable project.

52

A Rather Strange Living Room

A few of the many strange things: A picture is hanging upside down. The flowers on the wallpaper are upside down. There are fish in the television. A viking ship at sea and a witch on a broom are in the window. The sofa has a tie and a collar like a suit. It also has hands. The little table has two legs that are wearing lady's shoes. The other table has frog legs. Santa's treat is a decorated carrot. There is a watering can and a flower pot for his drink. The rockers on the rocking chair are going the wrong direction. There is grass instead of carpet on the floor. A flower is growing out of the rug and there is a snake around the rug. One of the stockings hanging at the fireplace is a foot. The numbers on the clock are wrong.

Find Someone Who

Get as much speaking practice as possible out of this activity by having students ask one follow-up question to each person who gives them a "yes" answer. In small groups or as a class, have students tell what they learned about their classmates.

53

Mystery Picture

Green Christmas tree with red ornaments.

54

Christmas Crossword Puzzle

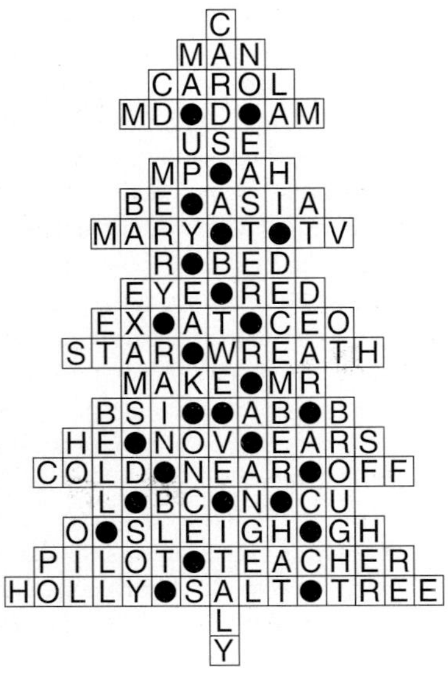

56

Christmas Party

A class Christmas party would be a way to combine songs, games, craft activities and recipes as well as present a performance of a Christmas play. *The Best Christmas Pageant Ever* referred to here is the original English title of the *Herdman* story (pp. 27–29).

58

Going Crackers

As there are 24, the jokes could be used in an Advent calendar, either alone or included in each of 24 Christmas crackers along with a small sweet and other surprise.

58/59

Christmas Decorations

Craft idea for young students: Pupils trace around one of their feet (with socks on) on brown paper and cut out the shape. Then on yellow paper, trace around both hands with fingers spread out. Cut out the hands and glue them to the top of the foot shape, gluing from the back. The hands are the antlers and the foot is a long face. Add a bright red circle for a nose and black paper circles for eyes. It's Rudolph!

60/61

A Taste of Christmas

The measurements have all been given in grams although in Britain recipes are traditionally given in pounds and ounces and in the US liquid and dry ingredients are measured in cups.

Wassail is also called Hot Apple Cider or Mulled Cider. In American English, cider is nonalcoholic apple juice.

63

Merry Quizmas

1C, 2B, 3B, 4B, 5A, 6B, 7C, 8B, 9A, 10B.

64/65

The Snowman

The recording gives a radio play version of this story. Because of the clear story line and large amount of dialogue and repetition, students can easily act out the story themselves, either following the exact words of the text or using their own words after reading/listening to the story. You probably have students in class who would enjoy making a video of the play which could be shown to other classes or at a parents' evening.

Reading/listening task:

List all the things in the story that are red.

66/67

The Cremation of Sam McGee

Before reading the poem, brainstorm the word *cold* and have students think of all the words and ideas they associate with it. Collect the words on the board and have students organize them any way they like. The questions on the student's page can be talked about either before or after reading the poem.

About the Poem:

1. The poem is a ballad. What other ballads do you know and what are typical characteristics of ballads?

2. How do the first eight lines set the mood of the poem? Why are these lines repeated at the end?

3. What words does the poet use to make the reader feel the cold?

4. How would this story be different if it were told as a short story and not with the strong, drum-beat rhythm and rhyme?

5. Note how the second accented syllable in each line rhymes with the fourth accented syllable. What effect does this extra rhyming pattern have on the rhythm of the poem? (Suggestion: it gives a stronger feeling of motion and drives the poem forward, like the sled across the snow; powerful, like a heartbeat).

69

Find the Differences

Be sure students don't look at each other's pictures when describing them and finding the differences.

Some of the differences:

An old man/young lady is skating. Two snowmen are fighting/are happy. A boy is pushing an old lady/snowman on skis. A boy has roller blades/ice skates. The boy is wearing earmuffs/a cap. He has a scarf/no scarf. There is a pocket/no pocket in his jacket. The old man is touching his hat/The young lady is touching her hair. A rabbit/seal is coming through the ice. A child is throwing Easter eggs/snowballs. A girl/boy is throwing them at a boy/girl. Two fish/ birds are flying in the sky. A (hot air) balloon/bunch of balloons is in the sky. There is a dinosaur/elephant near the trees. There is a duck/child under fir trees/palm trees.

70

Poems, Poems, Poems

This is a "pool" of poems to be dipped into as you like. Students could also receive a copy of the page and be challenged to choose one of the poems and memorize it. Small groups could work together on the longer poems and create a choral speaking version to present to the class or at a Christmas programme. Poems could also be copied onto Christmas cards, decorated with appropriate illustrations.

Snow Toward Evening and *Winter Morning* both contain snow metaphors (white petals and sugar, birthday cake icing). Before reading them, have students think of their own metaphors or similes: "What can snow be compared to?" "Snow is like …"

Creative writing activity:
Write the letters WINTER down the left side of a page. Begin each line with a word beginning with W, then I, then N, etc., each line having not more than four words. It's probably best not to call these acrostics "poems", or students will want to force them to rhyme, often using unnatural language.

Stopping by Woods on a Snowy Evening is one of the most popular American poems. Discussion points: Its rhyme scheme, what the speaker means by "promises to keep", what feelings are associated with sleep? death?, contrast the speaker who stops to contemplate the beauty of the woods with the horse who wants to move on and with the absentee owner of the woods. Just for fun, the poem can also be sung to the tune of "When the Saints Go Marching In."

MUSIC IN THE CLASSROOM

About the Recording

In order to create a typical carol-singing atmosphere, most of the songs were sung either a capella or with only a guitar accompaniment. Performers were students of the bilingual John F. Kennedy School in Berlin, Germany, as the intention was to have young people singing for their peers.

If they wish, students can of course sing along with the recording. However, it is sometimes more fun and more effective to first listen to the songs and then sing alone with a teacher or student as song leader. (Note: The music notation on the student pages is in an "easy" key. In some cases, the songs were recorded in a different key.)

Several songs on the recording are sung in *barbershop style*, a form of music which began in America in the 1890s. The barbershop was a meeting place where men not only discussed local politics while waiting for a shave and a haircut, but also sang together the popular songs of the day, often sentimental love songs and ballads.

Typical characteristics of the *barbershop style:* a capella, four-part harmony, a melody sung in a middle range with the other singers harmonizing above and below it, and choreographed movement. Women as well as men sing in this style, which is popular not only on many American college campuses but is propagated and encouraged by barbershop organizations in several countries.

Using Songs in Class

Song texts can be used like any other listening comprehension material:
– Choose 10–15 words or phrases from a song and put them in random order on the board. As students listen to the song, they put the words in the order that they hear them.
– Give students a copy of a song text in which some of the words are missing. It's easiest to do that with white correcting fluid. Students have to listen and fill in the missing words. Before listening to the song, they could speculate which words might belong in the "holes" and then listen to see if they were right.
– Put each line of a song on a separate slip of paper and mix up the papers. Students have to put the lines together like a puzzle. You could have students write the slips themselves and make up song puzzles for each other with different groups each getting a different song.

Some students may be interested in working in a small group and inventing a routine which involves co-ordinated hand and body movements that fit the words of a song. Students could either sing themselves or follow the example of pop singers and mime or lip-synch the words while the recording plays. You have to know a song very well to do this convincingly.

The Songs

Away in a Manger

26

This is often the first carol young children learn. Although written by an anonymous American in the 19th century, the publisher attributed it to Martin Luther either unknowingly or as a joke. Many songbooks today still perpetuate that bit of misinformation.

crib (AE) – *baby bed* **to low** – *to make the sound of a cow* **thee** – *(old use) you* **nigh** – *near*

Deck the Hall

18

(also: *Deck the Halls*) Old Welsh carol from the days when all the household servants celebrated Christmas together with the country squire and his lady in the hall of the old manor house. Before the singing and dancing began, a huge yule-log was brought into the hall and set ablaze.

to deck – *to decorate* ***bough*** – *branch* ***'tis*** – *it is* ***to don*** – *to put on* ***gay*** *(old use) – happy* ***apparel*** *(–'– –) clothes* ***to troll*** – *to sing heartily* ***Yuletide*** – *Christmas* ***Yule*** *= yule-log, see Christmas dictionary* ***chorus*** – *group of singers* ***measure*** *(old use) – round of dancing* ***to hail*** – *to greet* ***ye*** *(old use) – you* ***lad*** – *boy* ***lass*** – *girl* ***heedless of sth*** – *not caring or worrying about sth*

The First Noel

24

An English carol from the 17th century.

noel – *Christmas* ***deep*** – *(old use) late* ***intent*** – *plan* ***to draw nigh*** – *to come near* ***o'er*** – *over* ***myrrh*** – *plant substance used for making perfume* ***frankincense*** – *substance from trees which gives a pleasant smell when burnt*

Go Tell It on the Mountain

32

Well-known African-American spiritual.

God Rest Ye Merry, Gentlemen

18

One of the most popular English carols, it was heard in the streets of London as early as the 1700s. The first two lines are mentioned in Dickens's *A Christmas Carol* as being especially irritating to Scrooge. Musically, it is unusual for a carol to be in the Dorian (minor) mode.

to rest – *to keep* ***to dismay*** – *to make sb. feel sad* ***astray*** – *away from the correct path* ***tidings*** – *(old use) news* ***to comfort*** – *to help to sb. who is sad* ***blessed*** – *holy*

Happy Xmas (War is Over)

9

Written by John Lennon (1940–1980) and Yoko Ono (born 1933). In 1969 when people were demonstrating in the streets against the war in Vietnam, Lennon and Ono had thousands of posters printed and huge signs put up in major cities from Berlin to New York to Tokyo proclaiming "WAR IS OVER! If you want it. Happy Christmas from John and Yoko." Two years later Lennon recorded *Happy Xmas* with a children's choir from Harlem singing the "War is over …" slogan. The song was played extensively at Christmastime in 1980 after Lennon was murdered on December 8.

Jingle Bell Rock

68 🎧

Novelty song from the 1950s.

bushels of *– (AE sl) lots of* ***hop*** *– dance party esp. in the 1950s and 1960s* ***to prance*** *– to dance and jump around* ***to rock*** *– to dance rock 'n' roll* ***swell*** *– (old sl) good* ***giddyap*** *– said to a horse so it runs faster* ***to mingle*** *– to meet different people*

Jingle Bells

68 🎧

First published in Boston in 1857, written by John Pierpont, a Unitarian clergyman who also wrote patriotic songs for the South during the American Civil War.

When singing Jingle Bells with a group, everyone can make their own jingle noises to the rhythm of the refrain by either shaking bunches of keys or tapping plates or glasses with spoons.

o'er *– over* ***bobtail*** *– short tail* ***lean and lank*** *– thin and fit* ***misfortune*** *– bad luck* ***lot*** *– fate* ***drifted bank*** *– pile of snow* ***upsot*** *– upset, turned over*

Jingle Bells – Modern Version

Jingle bells, jingle bells, jingle all the way,
Oh what fun it is to go shopping every day.
Toy shop, book shop, department store, sports shop after that,
Gifts for all the girls and boys and don't forget the cat (meow!).

Dashing through the crowds, people everyplace,
Up and down the aisles, sneezing in my face.
It's so hard to choose, there's so much to see,
Wonder if what I got you cost more than you got me. Oh ...
Jingle bells, jingle bells, will they ever stop?
I've been shopping all week long, I'm just about to drop.
Ring the bells somewhere else far away from here,
We are really lucky Christmas comes but once a year.

Wrap your presents nice, pretty bows that shine,
Take them out to mail, you're gonna wait in line,
Fight your way back home, and if you are like me,
Maybe on the twenty-fourth you'll finally get a tree. Oh ...

Jingle bells, jingle bells, jingle dear St. Nick,
Got a hundred envelopes I'm gonna have to lick (yick!)
Jingle bells, jingle bells, my fingers all have cramps,
And to really top it all, I just ran out of stamps. Oh ...

Jingle bells, jingle bells, ringing in my ear,
I'll be broke till Easter-time, the same as every year,
Jingle bells, jingle bells, a few more days and then,
When I see the smiles I know I'll do it all again.

The Night Before Christmas

39 🎧

(Chopsticks version) The melody is based on Chopsticks, noted for being the tune that people who don't know how to play the piano know how to play on the piano. The Chopsticks tune was written in 1877 by a 16-year-old British girl, Euphemia Allen.

This is a shorter version of the poem than the original, but it includes the original beginning and ending, the part that native speakers remember and quote.

There are lots of parodies which use the rhythm pattern and opening line of this poem. Students might try writing their own version. Suggestion: *'Twas ten days before Christmas and all through the school ...*

O Come, All Ye Faithful

24 🎧

Often sung as the opening carol of a church service. Some books claim it is a Portuguese carol. Although it was first performed at the Portuguese embassy in London, it was translated from a Latin hymn and probably written by a member of a colony of English Catholic emigrants in France in the 18th century.

to behold *– to see* ***exultation*** *– great joy*

O Hanukkah

8 🎧

Well-known Hanukkah song based on a Jewish folk tune.

Once in Royal David's City

31 🎧

The songwriter, Mrs. C. F. Alexander, wrote nearly 400 hymns in her zealous attempt to make the doctrines of the catechism more appealing to children. This one is from her best-known book *Hymns for Little Children*. "Royal David's City" refers to the town of Bethlehem, traditionally considered the home of King David.

Rudolph the Red-Nosed Reindeer

33 🎧

(See also pp 34/35) First recorded by the singing cowboy, Gene Autry, in 1949 it was an instant hit and has remained one of the world's best-selling recordings. On the accompanying recording, the singers add the words "Yes sir it's ..." and "Those meanies".

The names of the animals on the page are puns. *Ewe* (female sheep) and *gnu* are pronounced like "you" and "new". *Wee* = small.

The Twelve Days of Christmas

45 🎧

Language note: a-swimming, a-milking, etc. are old forms which developed into the modern participle without *a*.

The first printed version of this song is from 1780, but it was already mentioned in the 13th century. The twelve days between Dec 25 and Jan 6 were declared a religious holiday in 567 by the Council of Tours. It was a time of feasting and gift-giving and it was considered bad luck to enter a house empty-handed.

One theory about the origin of the unusual gifts is that the first seven gifts were all birds which could be roasted and eaten. Even the *five gold rings* were once possibly five *goldspinks*, an old Scottish name for goldfinches. There are thus birds for each day of the old year and starting on the 8th day, Jan 1, the first human "gifts" arrive.

The song was often sung as a concentration game with each person singing one line. Whoever made a mistake had to forfeit something.

Lots of parodies have been made of this song, including a Hawaiian pidgin version about *two coconut, an' one mynah bird in one papaya tree*. Students may enjoy making up their own version with a collection of twelve unusual gifts.

The song can also be used for a mathematics activity. Have students figure out how many gifts were given altogether. On the first day, the singer's True Love gave one gift (a partridge), on the second day he gave three gifts (two turtle doves and a partridge), etc. On the twelfth day, he gave 78 gifts (12 drummers drumming, plus all the rest again).

Actually, this song can be seen as an example of medieval numerological wit. When the total number of gifts for each day are added together, it comes to 364, one for each day of the year until next Christmas.

Students could also figure out the patterns of addition and multiplication progression. When plotted on a graph, the result is a Christmas shape.

Performing the Twelve Days of Christmas

Acting out this song for an audience can be a lot of fun and offers an opportunity to get a large group participating actively.
There are four main characters who need to be willing to act expressively:
TRUE LOVE – "prince" costume
FAIR MAIDEN – "princess" costume
RING BEARER – tunic, tights, sash, carries a pillow with five gold rings sewn onto it
PARTRIDGE – colourful tail feathers, baseball cap with beak and crown feathers attached.
The rest of the students will have many different roles and will have to keep changing costumes and props very quickly. There should be at least twelve other students, but it is also possible with fewer. All performers should wear clothes of any solid colour.
Costumes, props and characteristics:
TURTLE DOVES: no special costumes needed, "fly" across stage hand in hand, FRENCH HENS: berets, CALLING BIRDS: cup hands around mouth and call "yoo-hoo", GEESE: roll plastic egg on floor, SWANS: wear white, "swim" across stage, MAIDS: carry buckets, LADIES: swirl colourful scarves, LORDS: leap, lifting legs high, PIPERS: play any kind of recorder or small flute, DRUMMERS: hit imaginary drums with drumsticks or chopsticks.
The song is sung by the audience at a slow tempo. They could either have copies of the song or students could hold up posters with the words. There should be a song leader and/or someone playing

the melody on an instrument, pausing where necessary.

As the audience sings the first verse, the action begins with True Love dramatically ringing Fair Maiden's (imaginary) doorbell and presenting her with a pompously strutting partridge. She is thrilled by the romantic gesture. As they sing "On the second day of Christmas ..." True Love again rings the doorbell, this time two turtle doves fly across the stage, followed by the strutting partridge. For each additional day the corresponding number of birds or people cross the stage, one group crossing from left to right, the next group from right to left, being careful not to run into each other. "Five" is always the same ring bearer. The higher the numbers get, the more the students will have to play different roles and keep switching costumes and props. This has to be planned and rehearsed carefully.

As the song proceeds, Fair Maiden is at first bewildered and then enraged by the quantities of birds and bodies in her house. The ring bearer becomes more and more terrified of approaching her with the rings. The action gets wilder and more chaotic. At the end of each verse, the partridge struts calmly across the stage. By the end of the song, Fair Maiden decides she may as well join in the fun and she leaps and drums and dances with them all. The last person on stage is the partridge. He bows and leaves.

We Three Kings

26

to bear *– to carry* ***to traverse*** *– to travel* ***yonder*** *– far away* ***plain*** *– flat land* ***to cease*** *– to stop* ***to reign*** *– to rule as a king*

We Wish You A Merry Christmas

3

When carol singers go from door to door singing, this is usually their closing song. Additional verses: *Now bring us some figgy pudding ... And bring it right here. We won't go until we get some ... So bring some to us now, We all like our figgy pudding ... With all its good cheer.*

Silent Night

Silent night, holy night,
All is calm, all is bright.
Round yon Virgin Mother and Child,
Holy Infant so tender and mild,
Sleep in heavenly peace,
Sleep in heavenly peace.

Silent night, holy night,
Shepherds quake at the sight,
Glories stream from heaven afar,
Heavenly hosts sing "Alleluia!"
Christ the Saviour is born,
Christ the Saviour is born.

Silent night, holy night,
Son of God, love's pure light.
Radiant beams from Thy holy face,
With the dawn of redeeming grace,
Jesus, Lord, at Thy birth,
Jesus, Lord, at Thy birth.

What's this?

Shtihl-luh nahkht, hye-lee-guh nahkht,
ahl-luhs shlehft, eyr-zahm vahkht
noor dahs trow-tuh hohkh-hye-lee guh pahr,
hohl-dehr k'nah-bun eem lohk-kee-guhn hahr.
Shlahf een heem-lihsh-ehr roo ...

"Silent Night" written so English speakers can pronounce it in the original German. Found in a music book used in American schools.

ADDITIONAL GAMES AND ACTIVITIES

Put Christmas Trimmings on Old Favourities

Merry Christmas Bingo

Write about twenty words on the board that have something to do with Christmas or winter. Choose them yourself or have students suggest them as you write. Have the students fold a piece of paper into sixteen boxes, four in each direction. Students write one word in each box at random so each paper is different. Distribute bits of coloured paper to use as markers. Read one of the words from the board and use it in a sentence. Students who have that word on their paper put a marker on that box. Continue until one student has a row of four words covered horizontally, diagonally or vertically. He or she shouts "Merry Christmas!" and is the winner. The winner could choose the words for the next round. Be sure students remove all markers from previous rounds. Variation: Instead of reading the words, give only a definition or description.

Snowman Hangman

Choose a Christmas word and put short lines on the board for each letter in the word. Students have to guess the word by guessing one letter at a time. If the letter is in the word, it is written on the corresponding blank line. If not, the leader begins to draw a snowman (instead of a hangman, as in the classic version). If the snowman is finished first, the leader wins and chooses another word. Otherwise the person who guessed the word can be the new leader. Draw the snowman in nine steps – three circles for body and head, two eyes, one nose, mouth, hat and broom.

Charades with Christmas Activities

Students act out in pantomime an activity relating to Christmas. If you wish, the student(s) doing the pantomime could begin by saying *Everyone's busy when Christmas is near, the busiest, happiest season of year.* Others: *What are you doing that keeps you so busy?* Player: *Watch me/us and see.*

Packing a Christmas Suitcase

Choose a sentence such as *I went Christmas shopping yesterday and bought ...* or *This year at Christmastime I'm going to ...* or *All I want for Christmas is ...* Students have to repeat items the others have said and add a new one. Variation: the items have to be in alphabetical order.

Alphabetical Gift Lists

Students can use dictionaries to write gift lists – the more unusual the better. *I'm giving my Aunt Annie an aardvark. I'm giving Bennie a box of beans and Charlie a cow, etc.*

Word Games

Make as many words as you can using the letters in *Happy New Year* or *Santa Claus* or *Merry Christmas.* Find as many Christmas words or expressions as you can that begin with each letter in the word Christmas. Write a sentence in which the first letter of each word begins with the letters of the word Christmas (or another word) in the correct order. Easier: Write a story in which the first letter of each sentence begins with the letters of the word Christmas in order.

Scrambled words

Using Christmas vocabulary or a few words from a song or text, scramble the letters in each word and have students unscramble them. Students may enjoy choosing some words from a text and scrambling the letters for their classmates to solve.

Variation: Keep the consonants in the correct order but remove all the vowels and try to guess the words.

Chain spelling

Using Christmas or winter words, one person suggests a word, for example "bell". The next person must find a word using the last letter in that word: bell, lights, star, reindeer, red ...

Who or What Am I?

One student chooses to be a Christmas object or person (snowman, star, angel, etc.). The others have to ask yes/no questions to find out who or what the student is.

Variation: Teacher writes a different Christmas object or person on stickers or slips of paper and sticks a paper on each person's back. Students have to go around asking yes/no questions to find out who or what they are.

Kim's Game

Display about 15 Christmassy items on a table where all can look at them carefully for two minutes. Then cover them up and students have to write what they remember.

Variation: Change the position of some items or add or subtract something. Students have to remember what has changed.

Show and Tell

Have students each bring one item to class to show and talk about. Items should all fit into one category. For example, something red, a Christmas decoration you made yourself, something Christmassy made in a foreign country, something you once got as a Christmas present. Besides just talking about them, students can also use their objects to play Kim's game (above) or set up a market and "sell" the items to each other. Or in groups of three, students have to make up a story using each of their three items in the story.

Letter Writing

Have students write letters to Santa Claus pretending they are a famous person – either an historical figure or current politician, TV star, singer, etc. They could also be a character from a fairy tale or other story. What would you ask Santa to bring you?

Some people like to write newsletters at Christmas that they photocopy and send to all their friends and relatives telling about what they have done during the past year. Have students write such a letter telling about their own year. They could also include information on current favourites – favourite music group, food, TV shows, books read, etc. The letters could either be real or imaginary.

Writing Topic

If you could give any gift in the world to any person in the world, what would you give to whom?

Things to Do with Old Christmas Cards

You'll need lots of Christmas cards for these activities, at least twice as many as the number of students in your class. Ask your friends in English-speaking countries to start saving their old cards for you!

* Spread out your collection and let everyone look at the cards. Each person chooses a card they especially like and/or one they especially dislike. Have them explain their choices in pairs or small groups switching groups after a few minutes.

* Play a variation of Kim's game. Put about ten cards on the floor or on a table. Let the students look at the cards for two minutes, then take them away and the students have to write down a short description of as many cards as they can remember. This could also be done orally in pairs.

* Spread out some cards at one end of the classroom. Students get into three groups at the other end of the room. When you say, "Find a card with ... (holly, Santa Claus, a house, etc.)", one person from each team runs to the cards and looks for that item. The first person who finds one gets a point for their team. Leave the cards on the floor/table after they have been chosen so there are always lots of cards to choose from.

* If you have plenty of cards, give each group of three to five students at least ten cards. The first group that finds the object you call holds up their card and gets a point. Some groups may not have a card for all the items you mention, but this doesn't matter. Make the language as easy or as difficult as you like depending on your class – from "Find a card with a Christmas tree" to "Find a card which looks like it could be an old painting."

* If you have cards from different countries, students could guess which cards they think are typical of which countries and explain their choices.

* Make a list of about five famous people – entertainers, politicians, etc. either contemporary or historical. In pairs or small groups, students choose which card they would send to whom and why. Or students themselves could think of famous people they would like to send their cards to and explain why. Students could also write a little letter and Christmas greeting to those people.

* In pairs, each student has one Christmas card and without showing the card to their partner they describe their cards to each other and try to find as many similarities (or differences) as possible.

* Again, without showing their cards to each other, one partner describes his or her card and the other has to draw it. Original and copy can then be compared and differences pointed out. If the class isn't too large, all the originals and copies can be mixed up and students have to decide which pictures go together.

* Each person gets one card and writes a description of it. The cards and descriptions are collected and mixed up. Students have to match up cards and descriptions.

* Each pair or small group receives about five to ten cards and has to put them into some kind of order. They have to decide on a system, for example from most beautiful to ugliest, from most old-fashioned to most modern, or from most serious to funniest. If possible, have students stick their cards in order on a piece of poster paper. Other students can guess what their ordering system was.

Christmas Sketches

On the board, write the titles of some suggested topics. Have the class discuss briefly what each sketch could be about. The students then divide into groups of three to five and each group chooses a topic, discusses a plot and begins to rehearse. (It's best if the sketches are NOT written down word for word.) The following day, the groups are given about ten minutes to rehearse a last time and then the sketches are performed before the class.

Suggestions for topics and possible situations:

Mrs Claus Changes Her Mind
After years of baking cookies and taking care of Santa's red suit, Mrs Claus decides she wants to deliver the presents and see the world.

Strike!
Led by Rudolph, the reindeer decide they would rather be eating cookies in front of a Christmas tree than waiting for Santa on a cold, slippery roof.

Santa Meets an Alien
While on his way to deliver presents, Santa and his reindeer almost crash into a UFO. They introduce the alien to the joys of exchanging presents and get a most unusual present.

Where are the Toys?
Two days before Christmas, the elves are shocked to find all the toys have been stolen. One clue is left behind in the workshop.

Christmas in July
Santa's elves trick him into thinking he has overslept by several months. They change his calendar from July 24 to December 24, wake him up, and send him rushing off to deliver presents to children in the middle of summer.

ABOUT THE WRITERS

Achenbach, Joel (born 1960 in Florida) graduate of Princeton University. He reads his commentaries on National Public Radio and writes a weekly column in American newspapers. (p. 40)

Brooks, Phillips (1835–1893) born in Boston, influential preacher and Episcopal bishop, most remembered for writing the words to the Christmas carol "O Little Town of Bethlehem." (p. 70)

De Angeli, Marguerite (1889–1987) born in Lapeer, Michigan. One of America's most popular writers and illustrators of children's books during the 1940's and 1950's. (p. 25)

De La Mare, Walter (1873–1956) born in Kent, England. His poetry and stories for adults and children often have an undercurrent of melancholy and mystery and reflect his fascination with a fantasy world of childhood. As an honoured poet he is buried in St. Paul's Cathedral. (p. 14)

Dickens, Charles see pp. 20–23.

Frost, Robert (1874–1963) born and raised in San Francisco, but much of his poetry deals with rural life in New England, where he later lived. One of America's most popular poets, he won the Pulitzer prize three times. (p. 70)

Fyleman, Rose (1877–1957) born in Nottinghamshire, England; singer, educator, editor, author of books, plays and poetry for children. (p. 3)

Gowar, Mick (born 1951 in London). Graduate of Cambridge University, taught communication and lifeskills, writes and performs songs and poetry for children and young people. (p. 44)

Henry, O. (1862–1910) pen name of William Sydney Porter, born in North Carolina, lived in New York City. Published over 250 stories and was the most famous short-story writer of his day. He wrote humorously and sentimentally about ordinary people. Typical of his style is the use of coincidence and a surprise ending. (p. 48)

May, Robert L. (1905–1976) lived in Evanston, Illinois; advertising executive and author. (p. 34)

Moore, Clement C. (1779–1863) born in New York City, see p. 39.

Nash, Ogden (1902–1971) American writer of humorous poems, famous for his outrageous puns, absurd rhymes and wildly assymetrical lines. (p. 70)

Poe, Edgar Allan (1809–1849) born in Boston. American poet and critic, famous as the first master of the short-story form. He lived a short and tragic life, which included the early deaths of his parents and wife and an addiction to alcohol and drugs. His poems are noted for an extraordinary manipulation of rhythm and sound. (p. 70)

Prelutsky, Jack (born 1940 in New York City). He has written many award-winning books of poems for young readers and has translated several books of German and Swedish verse into English. (pp. 44, 70)

Robinson, Barbara (born 1927 in Ohio). She has written several books and short stories for young readers. *The Best Christmas Pageant Ever* was among the American Library Association Notable Children's Books of 1971-75 and was produced as a television film in 1983. (pp 27–29)

Schulz, Charles M. (born 1922 in Minneapolis, Minnesota) American cartoonist, created the highly successful *Peanuts* comic strip in 1950. It began as a semi-autobiographical look at his own life as a constant "loser" like his hero Charlie Brown. (p. 13)

Service, Robert W. (1874–1958) born in Preston, England, grew up in Scotland, moved to Canada when he was 20. Worked for a bank where he was transferred to a branch in the Yukon. He was fascinated by the gold rush and many of his popular poems are about the trappers and prospectors who tried to make their fortunes there. (pp. 66–67)

Seuss, Dr. (1904–1991) pen name of Theodore Seuss Geisel, born in Springfield, Massachusetts. He added the "Dr" to his name "to sound more scientific," though he did receive an honorary doctorate in 1956 as well as a Pulitzer prize in 1984 for his enormous influence on children's literature in America. He wrote 48 books which sold over 100 million copies. *How the Grinch Stole Christmas* was written in 1957 and has become a classic, both in the picturebook and video version. (pp. 36–38, 43)

Strachan, Ian (born 1938 in Altrincham, Cheshire, England); worked in theatre, radio and television, author of several children's books.

Townsend, Sue (born 1946 in Leicester, England); mother of four, had worked at jobs such as hot-dog seller, community worker, and dress shop worker before writing her first enormously successful Adrian Mole book in 1982. (pp. 10-11)

Whittier, John Greenleaf (1807-92) born in Massachusetts of Quaker parents. A prolific and popular poet, deeply concerned with anti-slavery issues and social welfare, participated in founding the Republican Party in 1854. Much of his poetry celebrates his rural boyhood in New England. (p. 70)

Wordsworth, William (1770–1850) born in Cockermouth, England; leading figure in English Romanticism, noted for his simplicity of language in describing nature. (p. 14)

CHRISTMAS DICTIONARY

Advent From Latin for *arrival*, referring to the arrival of Christ. In Britain and the US the term is only used in a church-related context for the time including the four Sundays before Christmas. Advent calendars for children are becoming more popular in Britain, but they are not an essential element.

boar's head In the Middle Ages boar was considered a delicacy, and at Christmas a boar's head was decorated with garlands of rosemary and laurel and carried with much ceremony, singing, and trumpet fanfare into the great halls of the nobility. The tradition is still observed in parts of England, most famously at Queen's College, Oxford. They tell the story there that a student was once walking in the forest and reading a book when a wild boar attacked. With no time to draw his sword, the student stuffed his book down the boar's throat and choked him. He cut off the boar's head to retrieve his book and then triumphantly carried the boar's head into his college.

Boxing Day Dec 26, or the first weekday after Christmas. A public holiday in England, Wales, and parts of the Commonwealth. Churches used to have special boxes where people could put money for the poor. These boxes were opened after Christmas and the *box money* was distributed to the needy. Wealthy people also gave their servants gifts of money called *Christmas boxes* on this day. Tradesmen and apprentices used to collect tips in special boxes and postmen, dustmen, lamplighters, etc. were given *a box* or tip on the day after Christmas. Today, if a tip is given at all, it is given some time before Christmas. On Boxing Day there are many traditional sporting events, including horseracing and hunt meetings of foxhounds and horses. Many people also go to a *pantomime*, watch football matches, visit friends or simply relax at home.

candy cane A peppermint flavoured, red and white striped, hard sweet made in the shape of a walking stick or shepherd's crook. Americans sometimes hang them on the Christmas tree.

carol Used today to mean any Christmas song, although for some people a carol is only a traditional, not a modern, Christmas song. Historically, carols were popular, secular songs which were sung while people danced in a circle. People who go from house to house singing (and in Britain, often collecting money for charity) are carol singers or (AE) carollers.

chimney Santa's place of entrance on Christmas Eve. Nowadays not many people have traditional chimneys, but Santa manages to get in anyway. According to one legend, St. Nicholas threw coins down the chimney of three poor girls who had hung their stockings by the fire to dry and the coins fell into the stockings. Witches and spirits also traditionally entered houses through the hole in the roof made for smoke to escape.

Christmas From Old English *Cristes Maesse*, a mass or church service celebrated on December 25.

Christmas card Popular part of Christmas in the English-speaking world. Many people send about 50–100 cards to friends and neighbours and also use the cards to decorate their livingrooms. The first printed card was made in 1843. By the 1870s, the development of inexpensive colour printing techniques and a cheaper, more efficient postal system led to a boom in cards. Christmas cards and Christmas "newsletters" are also a popular way of keeping in contact with people in an increasingly mobile society.

Christmas pudding see p. 62. Also called *plum pudding* (an old-fashioned usage) as they used to contain dried plums.

Christmas tree Became popular in England in the 1840s when Prince Albert, Queen Victoria's German husband, introduced the idea to Windsor Castle. In appreciation for England's assistance during the war, Norway has sent a huge Christmas tree to Trafalgar Square in London every year since 1947.

cracker See p. 57.

Diwali A Hindu festival celebrated in late autumn, from a Sanskrit word meaning a row of lights. Houses are brightened with homemade lamps and colourful electric lights which welcome the return of Rama, a Hindu god, and show the triumph of light over darkness. New clothes, special foods, gifts, and fireworks are part of the festival, which is sometimes compared with Christmas.

eggnog See p. 61. Rum or brandy is often added.

evergreens People used to think that plants which didn't lose their leaves in winter contained special life-forces.

fairy, fairy lights In Britain, an angel-like decoration called a fairy is often put on the top of the Christmas tree. The little coloured electric lights on the tree are called fairy lights. (Real candles are very rare.)

Father Christmas Traditionally a tall old man with a holly wreath on his head who visited the Christmas celebrations in the great manor halls in England. Today he usually looks more like the American Santa Claus. The terms Father Christmas and Santa Claus are used interchangeably in Britain for the same giftbringer. Somehow, children don't get confused.

fruitcake A dark heavy cake made with nuts and dried and candied fruit.

grotto In Britain, a specially decorated area in a department store where children can come and talk to Father Christmas.

Hanukkah From a Hebrew word meaning dedication. A Jewish festival in December or late November. Dates change each year because it is based on a different calendar. In America, school and community programs often include both Christmas and Hanukkah songs and decorations. See pp. 6, 8.

"Happy Holidays" In American usage the *holiday season* means the time between Thanksgiving in late November and New Year's Day. In Britain the time around Christmas is called *the festive season. Happy Holidays* is a common greeting on American cards which can be sent to friends who celebrate Christmas, Hanukkah, or anything else in December. *Season's Greetings* is also used as a neutral greeting.

Hogmanay Origin of name unknown, perhaps from the Norman French version of *aguillanneuf*, a greeting for the last day of the year. Scottish name for New Year's Eve, an important festival there. See p. 6.

holly Evergreen plant with shiny dark green leaves and red berries used in pre-Christian days at midwinter festivals. The Church interpreted holly as a symbol of Christ's crown of thorns with the red berries as drops of blood.

ivy Plant used in traditional English Christmas decorations and mentioned in legends and songs. It could also tell the future. A girl would hold a leaf and recite "Ivy, Ivy, I love you; In my bosom I put you, The first young man who speaks to me, My future husband shall be."

Kwanzaa An African-American festival from Dec 26 to Jan 1. Although not celebrated anywhere in Africa, the festival includes some traditions, foods and symbols from various African harvest festivals. The name Kwanzaa is from a Swahili word meaning "first". On each of the seven days, a black, red or green candle is lit and one of the seven Kwanzaa ideals such as unity, creativity, and cooperative economics is stressed. The festival was first created in 1966 by Dr. Maulana Karenga, a professor of African-American history in California. It became more popular in the 1990s.

Messiah English form of Hebrew *mashiah*, the anointed, in Greek, *Christ*, the name given to Jesus by his followers. Handel's oratorio *The Messiah* is one of the most popular pieces of music performed at Christmastime in the US and in Britain.

mince pie See p. 62.

mistletoe *Mistle* may be related to German *Mist (dung)*, as the seeds are spread through bird droppings. *Toe* is from a word meaning *to branch off* (same as in *toe* of a *foot*). See. p. 14 and *The Chime Child*, pp. 15–17.

Nativity The birth of Jesus. A Nativity play is an enactment of the biblical Christmas story.

Noel From the French word for Christmas. Formerly used as a shout of joy in many songs and also for the songs themselves. Today the word is heard in the song *The First Noel* and is used decoratively on Christmas cards and decorations. (What's this? ABCDEFGHIJKMNOPQRSTUVWXYZ Answer: No L).

pantomime, panto A very British, very popular form of entertainment during the Christmas season. A pantomime is not a play without words, but a show with singing, dancing, jokes, and audience participation. The plays are based on traditional stories such as *Aladdin* and *Cinderella*. The ***Principal Boy***, the male hero, is always played by a woman and the ***Dame*** is played by a man.

plum pudding See *Christmas pudding*.

poinsettia Popular Christmas plant which Joel R. Poinsett (1779–1851), an American diplomat and amateur botanist introduced to the United States from Mexico, where the plant grows five metres high. Its large red flowers are really its top leaves; its real flowers are small and yellow.

Queen's (or King's) **Christmas message** At 3 pm on Christmas Day, the British monarch always speaks on TV to his or her subjects. It is broadcast throughout the Commonwealth.

reindeer Animals that pull Santa's sleigh through the air, probably from the idea that Santa is from a cold place in the North. See p. 39.

robin A red-breasted bird often pictured on British Christmas cards. While there are many legends about the popular bird (see p. 14), its use on Christmas cards can also stem from the red coats that English postmen used to wear and which caused them to be nicknamed *Robins*. A typical old Christmas card motif was a robin (bird) bringing a greeting in its beak.

Rudolph The most famous reindeer of all. See pp. 33–35.

Santa Claus From *Sinterklaas*, Dutch version of St. Nicholas, 4th century saint about whom there are countless legends (see *chimney*). Modern images of Santa were influenced by the poem *The Night Before Christmas*. See p. 39.

Saturnalia Roman winter festival: Some of its traditions were incorporated in Christmas celebrations.

Stephen, St First martyr of the Church, his Saint's Day is December 26. Legends about Stephen and horses (although it was probably a different Stephen) caused the day to be associated with horses and horse races.

stocking See *chimney*. At Christmas, specially decorated big stockings are hung either by the fireplace or, in Britain, also at the foot of children's beds. Santa fills them during the night with sweets and toys.

turkey Although native to Mexico, the name is based on a confusion with other "exotic" birds and the fact that foreign and unusual things often came from places in the east, including Turkey.

Twelfth Night Festival on January 6, 12 days after Christmas. Shakespeare's play *Twelfth Night* was written to be performed at the final day of this old 12-day festival. See teacher's notes about *The Twelve Days of Christmas* p. 76.

wassail from an old English greeting *waes haeil* "be healthy" formerly said when drinking a typical Christmas beverage, hot spiced ale with roasted apples. In Shakespeare's day, the word meant heavy drinking. Poor people used to wander through the streets at Christmas or *Twelfth Night* carrying a communal wassail bowl and begging for it to be filled, then singing carols in return. Today the term is used in the US as the name of a hot drink made with apple juice and spices. See p. 61.

winter solstice Darkest time of the year when the sun is farthest from the equator. Especially in northern regions, a time of rituals and festivals employing fire and light in an attempt to call back the sun.

wise men also called *magi* [ˈmeɪdʒaɪ], related to magician. In the Bible, St Matthew tells of wise men, probably meaning scholars who study the stars, who visited the Christ Child in Bethlehem. The idea that there were three of them, that they were kings, and that they arrived on Jan 6 developed much later.

wreath Circle of evergreens often hung on the front door or gate. While the wreath can be interpreted symbolically as a sign of changing seasons and the life-cycle, most people consider wreaths simply as the sign of a friendly welcome to Christmas guests.

wren A small brown bird. In Ireland, a symbol of betrayal. According to legends, during battles between the English and the Irish, the loud cry of the wren woke the English guards and caused the Irish to lose battles. On December 26 *Wren Boys* used to carry around a dead wren on a pole from house to house and get something to drink and eat. Later they carried a potato stuck with feathers, but today young people don't carry anything when they *Hunt the Wren*. See p. 6.

Xmas abbreviation for Christmas. See p. 9.

yule poetic or old-fashioned word for Christmas, from the name of an old Scandinavian winter festival, possibly related to a word meaning *to go around* (cf. Engl. *wheel*, Swed. *hjul*) referring to the turning of the year.

yule log in former times, a large log ceremoniously brought into the house on Christmas Eve and kept burning for 12 days. People believed the ashes had magic power to protect homes from lightning, cure diseases, and make fields and animals fertile. The nearly forgotten old custom of burning a yule log is being revived in ski resorts, hotels and pubs. A yule log is also a kind of chocolate cake baked in the shape of a log. See song *Deck the Hall*, p. 18.